# Waving Le Tricolore in the Land of Wales

## Claude Annik Rapport

# Dedication

Un grand Merci à toutes et à tous.


Diolch yn fawr.


Thank you so much for sixteen amazing years.

# Acknowledgements

I am grateful to Alex Falconer for her keen eyes and editing advice, to Eryl Samuel and Martin Rhys for their suggestions and sustained encouragement and to Michelle Emerson for shaping this book into its finished form.

My thanks go to Barbara Michaels, Val Spittle and to my daughter, Carolyn Clitheroe, for their support, and a very special thank you to my husband, Anthony, the best of "consorts", for his patience and understanding.

# Contents

# Voices in the Night

There is hammering at my front door.

At this rate whoever is responsible for the racket, and I am pretty sure he or she will be French, will smash the door down.

I can't find my housecoat.

"Coming, coming," I mutter under my breath, and curse Google for making my address available to anyone who takes the trouble to look up my name or function.

I brace myself for the man likely to be standing on my doorstep. "I lost my passport," he'll say, or "I've had my wallet stolen, and I've got to fly back to Paris tomorrow." Unless it's a distraught father whose ex-wife has taken their children abroad without his consent, or a young au pair girl bursting into tears as she explains the family didn't like her and threw her out after she cleared supper.

The banging grows louder, and I am surprised it has not woken up the neighbours yet. Or closer still, my husband. I hurry downstairs.

Large shadows press against the glass.

There is a heavy scuffle of feet.

"We need to get access," calls a man's deep voice.

No trace of a French accent. I am suspicious. I don't want to let anyone in.

I've heard how easy it is to be tricked, from internet scams to people falling prey to a request of help at the site of a fake accident; leave your house for a few minutes and return to find your jewellery and money gone. I wonder if I should pretend there's no one in, and phone the police.

"Let us in." The door shudders. With trembling hands I slide the safety chain in position, unlock the door, push my face close to the narrow opening, gasp, count to three to make sure I am fully awake, undo the chain, and open the door... to come face to face with three imposing firemen in full fire-fighting gear, complete with helmets, yellow jackets and black boots.

"I... I... didn't call you," I manage to stammer. "It wasn't me. I..."

The men stare back. "We know," replies the tallest one, "the police did."

"Yes, well... I did phone them for advice. I didn't know what to do about the fire... it was only small." It sounds like an apology. That's when I catch sight of the fire engine, a metal beast, bright red, all lights flashing, and it's parked at the top of the drive.

"So, what happened?"

I'm not sure which one of the three men spoke up but I've got to stop rambling.

"There was a half dozen youngsters playing at the back... behind the fence, late in the afternoon. They lit a fire, and I told them it was dangerous because of the oaks, and the line of old trees. They laughed at me, we had words, they turned unpleasant and I went back into the house."

"You checked the state of the fire after they left?"

"Well, I thought they had put it out, but when I looked out of my window on my way to bed there was an orange glow under the bushes. I wasn't sure if the gang of boys had returned so decided to ask the police what I should do."

Three faces frown back at me in unison.

"The sergeant I spoke to wasn't that helpful until I explained that according to the Vienna convention - the two words elicit blank looks - all diplomats, career or otherwise, are entitled to police protection should they feel threatened."

"I see." He may be trying to but I don't think he does. "And you felt threatened?"

"Yes I did."

"Right, that tallies," the firemen take a couple of steps forward. "They did say something about the security of the French Embassy." I cringe at the mistake, but I don't think now is the time to explain the difference between an Embassy and a Consulate.

"Better have a look."

Before I get a chance to explain that it would be easier if we went round the side of the house, heavy muddy boots trample all over the carpet. I take the men through the house, open the French doors and lead them to the back garden.

3

I can't match their purposeful strides. Their powerful torches light the way ahead but leave me in the dark. I miss a step, stumble, land on stubbly grass, and rub my knees. They are bare. And so are my legs. I curse under my breath. I've forgotten about my pyjama shorts and frilly top. I struggle to stand up, hurry forward. It's too late to worry about the impression I've made.

The men have reached the fence.

"There's a smouldering mattress down there." says their spokesman. "Could flare up at any time. We need water."

I don't expect them to follow me back through the house, to the kitchen, to the cold water tap, and ask for buckets. Buckets which they fill to the brim, carry out and empty over the fence a few seconds later to douse the fire. Three men moving as one, and with a certain elegance despite their bulk.

"That should do it." They wish me goodnight, hurry up the drive, climb back in their machine, and disappear down the road.

"What on earth happened here last night?" asks my husband the next morning on his way to get the paper from the front doormat. He points to large muddy footprints on the carpet.

"Ah, well, I can explain…"

# For Fear of the Guillotine

When it comes to football and rugby, all I can be sure of is that a lot of powerful looking men or women grab, kick, and chase a ball - round or oval - and get very physical and very muddy as they run around a pitch in front of large crowds who cheer, wave flags and banners, scream with joy or jeer in disgust at their favourite teams' performance. That I am not qualified to comment on the France/Denmark game is obvious to me but Karen from BBC Wales thinks otherwise.

"We were hoping you could come to the studio tomorrow morning and answer a few questions for *Good Morning Wales*," she explains when she calls. "Nothing searching, just general impressions."

"I'm so sorry," I tell her, which I am not, "but I shall be in Bangor attending the Queen's Golden Jubilee service at the cathedral."

"What a shame." Young Karen sounds disappointed. "Another time, maybe?"

"Yes, of course." It's a fib of no consequence, and she'll never know about my ignorance, will she?

The invitation, though, is real enough.

It stands proud on the mantelpiece in the sitting room. Embossed in black and gold, the words convey Her Majesty's wish that I should attend the morning service, accompanied by a guest of my choice. Knowing that mine is one of hundreds of such invitations does nothing to diminish the pleasure of having been asked, and like many a good republican, I am looking forward to the occasion. To the pageant the British are famous for. To seeing the Queen in the flesh. Never mind the long train journey to Bangor and wasting money on a hat I shall never wear again.

"That was a close call," I tell my daughter busy sewing a rogue button on her favourite silk top. "Imagine me having to talk about football! And going live on radio!"

We get busy with our packing. I line my new outfit - a navy and white suit, very French, according to my husband - with tissue paper before spreading it flat in my case. It would not do to appear in creased garments in front of the Queen - if I get that close that is. There remains, of course, the problem of carrying "the" hat, the fragile, yet bulky and necessary appendage to such an expedition. I like the idea of a hat box but with only two hands at my disposal - my daughter has her own mini-wardrobe to see to - I settle for a large plastic bag, not as elegant, but easier to contend with.

Next morning, we are up early and at Cardiff Central Station well before the train is due. It's an uneventful journey through the heart of Wales; fields run past the window, here and there the spire of a church in a village we can only guess at, and for four and a half hours the sonorous breathing of the bulky man slumped on the itchy banquette in front of us.

By the time we reach Bangor it's early evening, and I look forward to the comfort of the country B&B we shall be staying in, where - according to the guide book - we can be sure of superior accommodation, good home cooking, peaceful surroundings and a warm welcome.

At first glance, in his baggy cords and home-knitted jumper, our host looks the genial type, but he doesn't offer to help with our bags and there is no cup of tea with which to greet the weary travellers. As for the room we've been allocated, it looks worn, tired, grubby: limp curtains, faded counterpanes, ill-matched towels dumped on non-identical twin beds. Worse, colonies of long departed flies have chosen the window ledges as their final resting place. My daughter pulls a face.

"It can only get better," I tell her in a mild attempt at humour, and we get busy with damp tissues, get rid of the small corpses, wipe the dressing table clean, and check the state of the toilet. Just in case. Once we've hung our clothes in the wardrobe, and freshened up, we make for the dining room in search of our evening meal - which proves to be worse than ordinary. Still hungry when we leave the table we decide we might as well venture into the town, a short taxi ride away, and spend the rest of the evening in the comfort of a welcoming pub.

I am just about to dial the cab company's number from the discomfort of the dark and diminutive lounge reserved for the guests, when our host rushes forth.

"Oh, I forgot, there is a message for you. From the BBC." He sounds impressed. "They'll ring back at eight."

I frown, wondering how they managed to find me.

"... and your husband phoned, not long afterwards." He pulls a scrap of paper out of his jacket pocket and looks around as if lost. "Excuse me, I need my glasses." He retrieves them from the dresser, peers through the thick lenses, and starts again. "He said he was sorry but he had no choice

about giving the phone number. He spoke to
Karen. Very insistent. And have a lovely time."
He hands me the note and shuffles away.

I am tempted to ignore the message from
young Karen - I think of her as long-legged, blonde
and in her early twenties - but I know I shouldn't.
Anyway, I give myself a smile in the hall mirror; I
am miles away from the Cardiff studio. She can't
get at me. I am safe.

The phone rings on the dot of eight.

I have underestimated the tenacity of the girl,
all smiles, I know, even though I can't see her.

"I've had a word with my colleagues in
North Wales," she explains once the niceties are
out of the way. "I don't know why I didn't think
about it before but of course we've got a BBC
studio in Bangor," she is very pleased with herself,
"so there won't be a problem..."

"I'm not sure that I..."

"...for you to take part in the broadcast."

I twist the telephone flex with my free hand
and, for a split second, am visited by a murderous
thought. You are wrong, I am tempted to shout at
her, there is a problem: I know less than nothing
about football and I have no wish to make a fool of
myself. I must tell her.

"The thing is..."

9

She ignores me. "We'd like to go on air just after seven."

I grimace at the same mirror that saw me smiling a few minutes ago.

"I don't think you realise..."

Once again, no reaction. I suspect she is pretending she cannot hear me.

"I'll get someone to open up the building. I'll call you when you get there... and don't worry, I'll organise your taxi from here. Speak in the morning. Bye."

I don't get a chance to say, to shout, that she's wrong. There is plenty for me to worry about. I am seething, and she has ruined my evening.

Tempted as I am to hide in our room until morning, my daughter insists that it won't do any good and that we should go out for a drink.

"Don't pull such a face. You should have been more assertive, told her you didn't want to do the interview. You and your sense of duty."

She is right, of course, yet it is Karen I blame for the panic that has me hunting for discarded newspapers in the waste bin of the pub where I seek refuge with my daughter, Karen I hold responsible for my third whisky and ginger, Karen who forces me into making endless lists as soon as I get back to the B&B: names of referees, trainers, coaches, club captains, and players, of course, together with the injuries they might have suffered, not forgetting their possible replacements. I jot down pitch conditions, who plays best in what, and check on the weather forecast. So much information, my head is buzzing. As for the bed I am supposed to sleep in it is littered with articles I've cut out with nail scissors, and still there is more for me to try and commit to memory.

"Mother, switch off the light, I can't sleep!"

I am forced into the bathroom, where I nest half the night on a musty blanket I found at the bottom of the wardrobe.

Three hours' sleep leaves me thick headed and with the feeling I have just flown in from a faraway continent. By the time I have showered, scalded my mouth with a few sips of scorching tea - no milk on the hospitality tray - dabbed a little makeup on my cheeks, and pinked my lips, the taxi is waiting in the silence of the early morning.

"BBC studio?" asks the driver as I climb into his white Mercedes.

"Yes." I don't do nice at 6.30.

He taps the clock on the side of the dashboard. "I doubt they'll be open that time of the morning."

"There will be someone there, take my word for it." It would not occur to me to doubt Karen's efficiency for one minute. I pat the bundle of notes I stuffed in a large envelope, close my eyes and try and recall the names of the French team.

"French, are you?" asks the driver.

I nod.

"I bet you'll be watching the match."

Suddenly inspired I move forward to the edge of my seat. "Do you know anything about football?"

"Used to play when I was younger. I tell you what," he looks at me in his rear mirror, "that team of yours can turn pretty dozy. Just as well they no longer use the guillotine, there wouldn't be a head left in place." With the side of his hand he chops off imaginary heads. Under normal circumstances he would make me smile, but not today.

I climb a few steps, ring the doorbell. No sign of life. If nobody lets me in... I let my mind scuttle towards a pleasing conclusion... I can't do the broadcast. That's when I notice that the door is not flush with the jamb and when I push the wooden panel it offers no resistance. I step inside the dark hallway.

"Anyone there?" Three times I throw the question at the empty space. On the reception desk a sheet of yellow A4 catches my eye. *Claude, please go into room 4, down the corridor first on the right.*

Hardly have I stepped in and the phone rings. "Karen?"

"Good morning. Slept well?"

Such a ridiculous question does not deserve an answer.

"I'll talk you through what we expect of you."

"Shouldn't I wait for whoever is going to do the interview with me?"

"Ah..." I don't like the sound of that inflated vowel. "I suppose I should have said that, well, actually you will be on your own."

"On my own?"

"Yes. Sorry about that."

"I don't think..." but that is not true, I am thinking fast, "I don't think I can do the interview on my own, so..."

"Nothing to worry about. Trust me."

And there follows explanations as to the distance between mouth - mine - and microphone, voice - mine - not too loud please - the cues, and the importance of keeping the headphones on - they smell of hair cream - at all times.

"When the red light flashes you'll be on air, so try not to rustle paper or cough or make a loud noise. Got that?" She assumes that I have. "One last thing," I hear voices in the background, "the wall clock in front of you should read 6.50. Ten minutes to go."

I make that 600 seconds. I spread my notes on the table, take a few deep breaths and try to fool myself all will be well. The red light flashes and stares at me, unforgiving. A slight crackle in my ears, and a voice, young, male, assured.

"I will introduce you first... then bring you in every few minutes. Please keep your answer reasonably short."

As if I am likely to have much to say. My palms stick to the table, my neck throbs, and I need to rub the ache out of my temples but, of course, I can't. No sooner have I dealt with one question than I have to field another, none of them easy or mundane as I was promised, and if it weren't for my night's work I doubt I would have had anything to say. But speak I do, in an echoey sort of voice I barely recognise; I borrow comments, steal opinions, risk a little humour, cast furtive glances at my notes as if I could be spied on, and at long last the red light goes off. I sit very still, close my eyes, and listen to the silence deep inside the headphones.

As soon as I am free of the plastic shackles I feel lighter, liberated and let out a very loud, "Yesss!" I pick up my notes, throw them in the air, watch as they drift down and land on the ground. A quick sweep to gather the lot in an untidy bunch, and in the waste paper bin they go. Time now for a short victory dance round the room, followed by a little chanting. "I did it! It's over." Never mind if I look ridiculous, nobody's watching.

I grab my bag, hurry out of the building, climb inside the awaiting taxi and am tempted to wave at passers-by as we drive through the streets of Bangor.

"So?" asks my daughter too anxious to listen to the programme. "How did it go?"

My smile says it all.

"Well done you!"

She zips me into my dress, checks the angle of my hat and hands me my gloves. We are ready. It is a 10-minute taxi ride and a short walk through the crowds to the cathedral. We produce our invitation cards, step over the threshold into the cool of the building, follow the ushers, take our seats in the south nave, acknowledge acquaintances who, like us, have travelled from Cardiff, and wait for the service of Thanksgiving to begin.

Promptly at 11. With the slow processing of the cathedral choir, and members of the clergy who swish past in their richly coloured robes. From outside a muted roar heralds the arrival of Her Majesty the Queen and His Royal Highness Prince Philip, who are received by the Dean of Bangor and greeted by a fanfare of trumpeters before being led to their seats.

The service flows on, from anthems to prayers, from gospel readings to moments of reflection, from voices rising high to intervals of deep silence. By the time the organ voluntary bursts forth, I have almost forgiven young Karen for my early morning ordeal, all thoughts of the guillotine have vanished, and I am happy to share the cheering of the well-wishers with Her Majesty when she stands outside the cathedral.

# It is an Honour

"Don't worry it's just been sent, recorded delivery. I took it to the post office myself. You're bound to get it in the morning." I imagine the woman, all smiles behind her London desk. She will forget my call, move on to another task, and leave the fretting to me.

Throughout the night I keep waking in and out of anxiety dreams, packing bottomless cases, running after planes, searching for tickets in pockets deep with holes. I am up early waiting for the postman, who turns up on my doorstep minutes before my lift is due to arrive.

"Going somewhere nice?" he asks, taking in the black suit, the pink silk shirt and the Hermès scarf tied casually round my neck.

I reply that I am, sign the chit he hands over, and in exchange, he presents me with a thick, padded envelope stamped with the French Consular seal.

"Nice car that," he says. I turn round and watch an old classic navy jaguar roll slowly down the drive and purr to a stop outside my front door.

"I hope I have not kept you waiting?"

I assure Major Jones that he hasn't, before climbing inside the car, all cream leather seats, walnut veneer, the faint smell of pipe tobacco, and a hint of peppermint.

The heating is full on and the conversation slow. Like the traffic. Unusual for a Tuesday morning.

"Must be an accident somewhere," remarks my companion in the clipped tone of a retired army man. "Still, not to worry, I have allowed for such an eventuality, and I have been given detailed instructions on how to get to Corporal Lewis' house. A delightful old gentleman. Such an honour for him to be awarded the *Légion d'Honneur*."

"Well deserved I believe, a courageous man." I have read about David Lewis, about his escape from Nazi Germany dressed as a nun, about the parachute jump in a small French village and the way he dangled from the church spire until the local fire brigade managed to free him. "I am really looking forward to meeting him. He sounds like quite a character."

"He certainly has plenty of stories to tell." A dry little cough. "I take it that you have brought the medal. I believe there was some confusion as to where it should be sent."

I pat the envelope that sits on my lap, feel the rectangular box inside and smile my reassurance.

"I remember once having been given the wrong medal." He clutches the steering wheel a little tighter. "Very embarrassing for all concerned."

I sit up. I feel a little queasy. I should have checked. What if the box is empty?

A shiver runs down my back.

I resist the urge to rip the envelope open, and force myself instead to run a finger under the flap. I ease out the box. It's red, the right colour. I hold it, take a breath, slowly raise the lid, and can't help smiling at the silver medal, enamelled white, and decorated with an enamelled laurel and oak wreath. It rests on a bed of white satin. I caress the red ribbon the medal will hang from when I pin it to the chest of the old gentleman being honoured today, and experience a sense of awe. The decoration carries so much meaning to me and the French child I once was. I close my eyes and let myself be carried back to the classroom of my childhood where I breathe in chalk, ink and burning wood.

I am 10 and it's nearly home time, but before the class can be dismissed there is the short Saturday morning ceremony to be performed.

19

*Mademoiselle* calls us to order, waits for our loud
whispers to die down, for our tightly laced-up feet
to stop shuffling, and our inky hands to settle flat
on our desks. "You've worked very hard this week,
all of you, but some of you deserve to be singled
out for your excellent performance." She smiles at
us from behind her desk and beckons Nicole to join
her on the wooden platform.

I try not to envy my best friend who, flushed
with pride, returns to her seat with the *Médaille
d'Honneur*, a military style cross, with navy blue
and white enamel rising from a gold background.
She carries it on the cushion of her open palm and
goes back to her seat. Odile is next, and even
though her medal, green and silver this time, looks
more modest I would pin it with joy on the lapel of
my best coat, the one I have to wear to my
grandmother's for the ritual Sunday lunch. Maybe
then she would kiss me on the forehead, the way
she does my cousin Henrietta, a studious child, be-
medalled on a weekly basis of course, and destined
for great things according to *Grand-Mère*.

"I gather it was an order created by
Napoléon?"

"Pardon?" The question has me rushing back
to the present. "You're right. All orders of chivalry
were abolished at the time of the French revolution

and it was Napoléon's wish that merit should be recognised, hence the creation of the *Légion d'Honneur*, a secular institution established in 1802 to honour both soldiers and civilians."

I gently close the lid of the box, and we remain silent until he slows down.

"Nearly there."

A couple of bends and we pull up in a private car park.

"Shall I look after it for you?" He reaches out for the boxed *Légion d'Honneur* with a gloved hand. "You'll be busy meeting people." For a split second I think he might have read the coveting in my eyes, and how reluctant I am to let go of the medal.

As soon as we open the car doors I am blinded by the flash of cameras and my companion escorts me up some steps to a kind of terrace lined with narrow houses, recently built, the red bricks the only splash of colour on the grey background of the slag heaps.

The front door is wide open, and never have I seen so many people packed in so a narrow a hallway: standard-bearers, their thick leather belts cutting into their waists, a medley of ex-soldiers, TA, Regular, wearing uniform jackets complete with rows of medals that tinkle as they move, old

men in shiny shoes, and hands cupped at the ready
to better channel the voices round them to ears
tufted with white hairs.

What few women there are have congregated
in the kitchen, where I imagine them busy slicing
and buttering bread ready for sandwiches, warming
sausage rolls, and driving sticks in cheddar cubes
topped with pineapple.

"Excuse us please, let the Consul through."
The loss of the Honorary does register but if they
want to lend me more importance for the occasion
I see no reason for correcting them.

We've made it to the living room,
overflowing with family members, children,
grandchildren, and great grandchildren, all on their
best behaviour. Friends too. Lots of them. At the
age of 94, no doubt one of the few men of his
generation still alive, David Lewis strikes me as a
popular man.

Major Jones is by my side. "Corporal Lewis,
let me introduce you to the representative of the
French Government." He is right of course, but at
this rate I run the risk of thinking myself more
important than I am. As long as they don't get me
mixed up with the Ambassador and refer to me as
'Your Excellency' I'll be fine.

The Corporal is shorter than I am. His suit on the big size for his frame, the stiff collar of his white shirt digs in the crêpe folds of his neck, the sleeves need shortening, and I can just detect the braces that hold his trousers in place.

And yet I can still see the child he once was, despite the dentures edged with overly pink gums, the web of wrinkles that line his lips and the dry papery skin of his hand as he shakes mine. It's the glint in his eyes, his smile, his apparent ability to enjoy the moment.

We get into position. Short of denting the ceiling, the standard-bearers have to compromise; they secure the poles in their holders, unfold the embroidered ensigns and raise them as high as they can. David Lewis stands by my side.

One voice at a time the room falls silent, and I wish someone would open the window and let in some air.

"If you'd like to go ahead with the ceremony…" whispers the Major.

"Fine." I can hardly hear my own voice.

It's the tension, the anxiety at the thought my speech might not fit into the right grooves, for I know it will be played and replayed in the minds of those present, especially the old soldiers, for all the years they have left to live.

The speech goes down well. I wanted to be moving but not without humour; it would not have suited the man who is being honoured today. He trembles a little. "Are you all right?" I whisper.

"Yes, thank you." He rests a hand on my arm, "I liked what you said, but I never felt I'd been all that brave, you know, we just did what had to be done."

I squeeze his hand. "Shall we proceed with the medal?"

He nods.

Major Jones opens the box and presents it to me. Never mind this is my fifth time. I feel as moved today as I have on the other four occasions. Privileged to share in the glory, humbled and so very proud. It more than makes up for the *Médaille d'Honneur* I never pinned on my coat lapel all those years ago.

"Ladies and gentlemen, the time has now come for me to pronounce the very special words which, together with this medal," I offer a glimpse of it to the gathering, "will confer the highest Honour France can bestow upon a man or a woman of great worth."

The recipient and I face each other. "I shall begin with the English translation. In the name of the President of the French Republic, and with the powers which I have been granted this day, I declare you to be a knight of the *Légion d'Honneur*."

The audience holds its breath.

I pick up the medal, not that heavy when I reflect on the recognition of excellence it embodies. My hand doesn't look that steady.

"Corporal David Lewis," he blinks to hold back the tears, "*au nom du Président de la République française, et en vertu des pouvoirs qui nous sont conférés nous vous faisons Chevalier de la Légion D'honneur.* "

With care, I drive the double pronged pin through the thick cloth of the old soldier's jacket, pat the ribbon in place, embrace the new *Chevalier*, take a step back and hold his hand in both of mine.

"Congratulations."

From silence to an avalanche of sounds: voices, laughter, a toddler screaming, the bursting flash of the photographer's camera every few seconds, corks released from bottles of fizzy wine.

It is over a tray of egg and cress sandwiches that Corporal Lewis asks me what I think of the view over the valley from his living room.

"Lovely," I say, and chew as delicately as I can. "Must be glorious in the summer."

"It's even better from upstairs."

"Is it really?" I can't see that it could look that different, but still, now is not the time to be ungracious.

"Go and see for yourself, second door to the left, past the bathroom. It's well worth it." He nudges me forward and I don't want to offend.

Several pairs of eyes follow my every movement as I climb the flight of stairs.

The bedroom is a good size and very much what I expected: the white counterpane pulled taut over the double bed, a pair of tartan slippers waiting on a half-moon rug, an alarm clock ticking away on an old-fashioned side table, and faces that stare back at me from family photos hanging on the walls.

I walk to the window, pull back the net curtain, press my nose against the glass and yes, the view is pleasant, but no different from the one framed by the living room window.

Is it my imagination or do I see a grin on the new *Chevalier's* face when I reach the hallway?

"Very nice," I tell him, "I can understand why you like living here."

"Yes, lovely place," he chuckles, "and I hope you don't mind…?"

"Don't mind what?" I wonder if it's his age.

"Asking you to go upstairs." The grin spreads all over his face, and at the same time he manages to look embarrassed - the little boy face again.

"The thing is," a friend of his steps forward, "he won't want to tell you but you must be wondering, and you've been such a good sport like…"

"Yes?"

"We had a bet, you see."

"What sort of a bet?" I am totally confused by now, not even sure why I am asking questions at all.

Corporal Lewis grins and turns to me.

"You shouldn't be offended," the loose flesh round his neck quivers a little, "but I bet this lot," he grins at his friends as if in need of their support, "I bet that even at the grand old age of 94 I could still get a good looking woman in my bedroom." He takes a breath. "And I won!"

# Surprise Baby

"Hello, *bonjour*." She hesitates. "Do you speak French?"

"*Oui, bien sûr.*"

She is relieved, she tells me, because her English is a bit shaky, particularly on the phone.

"How can I help?"

"I want to register my baby, and apply for an identity card for him but someone told me I had to go to London."

"There's no need, we can do it here."

My next question is to ask her where she lives. "Merthyr Tydfil." A rather impoverished, depressed sort of town, 25 miles north of Cardiff, on the way to the Brecon Beacons. She adds she doesn't have a car.

It will be a long journey to Cardiff, first by coach, then she will have to catch the bus to my part of town on the edge of the city, and all that with a baby likely to need feeding or changing.

"Any chance of someone giving you a lift?"

"No," she says, "...my boyfriend..." she hesitates, "the baby's father... he's in... he has... he isn't available."

"No friends with a car?"

"Not really. I don't get to meet many people on the estate."

While listening to my caller I wonder if her predicament would justify my driving to Merthyr, but next week threatens to be over busy. Better not make a commitment I may not be able to honour. I can always phone her back if there is a change of plans.

"What would you suit best?" No doubt she is eager to take the new baby to France to meet her family. "Morning or afternoon?"

"Tuesday about lunchtime, if that's alright with you?"

"Fine." I keep quiet about my unwritten rule of no appointments until 5.30. We agree she will be with me at 1, 1.30 at the latest. "I'll be waiting for you." I should be able to take her back to the station but I don't tell her, just in case I have to disappoint her.

"You've got all the necessary documents?" She assures me she has, and after an exchange of *"au revoirs"* we put our respective phones down.

On Tuesday mornings I like to go for a swim, and today I am running late. Wet hair wrapped in a towel I rush back from the pool with 10 minutes to spare, relieved not to find my visitor standing in the porch, waiting for me.

I am making toast when I pick out a timid knocking at the door.

She's only a youngster, 18, 20 maybe, still plump in the oversized jumper that reaches almost to her knees. Her long dark hair is tied back in a low ponytail, and her face, open and friendly, is free from makeup.

No baby with her, though, so I assume mother and child were given a lift after all and that whoever drove them down is looking after the little one. There is a play area at the bottom of my road, and I don't suppose they'll be long.

"Do sit down," I tell the young mum. "It shouldn't take more than 20 minutes or so."

I look through the documents she brought with her, hunt for a black biro - blue is not acceptable, it doesn't photocopy well - and notice her anxiety when I present her with the form she needs to fill in.

"Don't worry, I'll guide you through." I take a seat next to her. "Best to deal with the signatures first. Yours of course, as you are applying for an identity card on behalf of your child. It's a bit tricky. One of them has to fit in that space." I point to the narrow little box which I framed with strips of pink post-it notes at the top of the document.

"Make sure the second signature at the bottom of the page matches the one at the top."

I push a small pad towards her. "Try it out first." Fortunately she is not a "scrawler" and a couple of attempts later she is confident enough to complete the task.

Filling in the rest of the form is easy: name, first name - the child's - parents' names, address; just a short hesitation over place and date of birth.

"Good." I put the document safely away.

"Oh, I nearly forgot, you'd better let me have the little one's birth certificate, and the photographs of course."

A look of surprise spreads across her face. "The photographs?"

"Not to worry. You can send them to me."

"The thing is …"

She is going to tell me that she tried with a digital camera but that she did not manage it, or that the baby wouldn't sit still long enough in the photo booth of her local supermarket.

"I know, it's not easy to take a picture of a very young child."

She neither agrees nor disagrees.

"The best thing to do," I continue, "is to lie the little one on the floor. A white blanket or sheet makes a good background."

She nods.

"Will they be here soon?"

"What do you mean?"

"I take it that the friend who gave you a lift is looking after the baby."

"I came by train and bus."

"But I assumed you knew that I have to see the child to check for likeness when I get the photographs."

"You can't." She pats her stomach, and grins at me. "I'm not due for the C-section for another two weeks."

# Child Play

"I'll come up later," I said to my yawning husband. "Won't be long."

Tired as I was, I felt the need to stretch time to better appreciate the peace and quiet of the evening. I looked forward to a little television and a few pages of a good book, which hopefully would be followed by hours of uninterrupted sleep - unless the local cats resumed their territorial in-fighting.

It was raining. Gusts of wind whispered down the chimney, a comforting background for the woman caught in a nightmare on the screen; in and out of rooms she ran, but somehow her pursuer trapped her in the kitchen, and blood splashed all over the beech units when he plunged his knife in her chest.

I grabbed the controls and put an end to the woman's agony. I like my crime stories to begin post-murder; gore isn't for me, it gives me nightmares.

Before turning off the downstairs light I walked into the dining room, renamed the Consular Room, and sat at the table. I set the late afternoon's passport applications and associated forms into three piles, ready for the final check in the morning. I scribbled a reminder to myself that one of them was incomplete, glanced at the answerphone in case I'd missed a lone message, and was about to close the door when I spotted a teddy bear lying on his back on the parquet floor. It cried a mechanical wail when I picked it up to rest it on the button-backed chair. Another look at the soft bellied animal. No, it had not escaped from the small box of toys I keep under the piano when attempting to keep the peace with toddlers.

I recalled the afternoon's appointments: an elderly lady, recently widowed and drowning in paperwork, a young Erasmus student who had lost his ID card, and an exhausted mum, lank hair, ash circles under her eyes, and the haunted look of the sleep-deprived. The bear must have belonged to one of her sons, four boys in muddy trainers, and blessed with the gift of kicking. I would phone her in the morning, ask if she wants me to post the teddy or maybe she could pick it up on the way back to North Wales. "I can't face the 5-hour drive back home in the dark," she'd said, "not on my own with the boys. We'll stay at my mother's, she doesn't live far away. They haven't seen her for months."

I made a mental note to request the presence of a second adult next time I was threatened by the *en masse* visit of under 10s.

Lights off, time for bed.

By the time I completed my nightly ablutions and slipped into bed, my husband's snoring had reached a sort of musical fullness, notes escalated, hovered, descended, only to rise again and squabble at the back of his throat. I patted his shoulder, tried a little whistling, whispered that he might be more comfortable on his side, all to no avail, and after a brief pause the snoring took flight again. Counting sheep was futile, I knew that, and so would plugging my ears with little balls of wax. Regretfully, I picked up my pillow, pecked my husband on the cheek, and tiptoed toward the spare room.

I let the pale light of the moon guide me towards the single bed. Some small spiky objects surprised my bare feet. Odd. The room had been hoovered early in the day. I reached out for the side light, switched it on and studied the floor. Where there should have been nothing but uninterrupted sand stone carpet, lapping at the feet of a set of pine bookshelves, small islands of foil wrappers had surfaced and released pebble-like objects, some whole, others crushed to the size of thick breadcrumbs. I squatted, looked more closely. No doubt about it, a small knife or possibly a fingernail had freed a month supply of anti-cholesterol tablets.

Some were missing. 10, possibly more. I hunted under the bed, around the room, pulled out a few books, scanned the shelves.

Nothing.

It must have been one of the boys this afternoon. I seemed to remember losing sight of the 4 year-old while I busied myself taking his brothers' finger prints for their new I D cards.

Getting through to my local hospital at night proved more difficult than I had thought, and it was midnight by the time I got to speak to a knowledgeable young duty doctor.

"It won't kill him," he reassured me "but you should warn the parents that he is likely to throw up throughout the night, in fact it may already have started."

Great. I didn't voice the comment. "Anything they can do?" I asked

"No, not really, just tell them to keep him off chocolate for a few days, give his liver a rest." His beeper went off, seconds before the rushed goodbye.

The next voice I heard shook a little with age, and no doubt, anxiety. I imagined the house in darkness, the grandmother knocking over a glass of water on the bedside table as she reached out for the phone.

"Who's that?" she asked

I explained who I was.

"What do you want?"

"Do you think I could have a word with your daughter?"

"Florence," the old voice called out, "there's a woman on the phone…"

I sat on the edge of my bed, twirled the flex with my fingers and rehearsed what I was going to say.

"Go back to bed, Mother, I'll deal with it." The phone changed hands. "Yes?"

"So sorry to bother you at this time of night but…"

"I take it what you have to say can't wait until the morning?"

"Well, not really, what I mean…" I started babbling. "If you recall…" my prepared speech deserted me. "If you remember, you came to see me this afternoon and…"

"Of course I remember."

37

"I believe your youngest son went up to my bedroom and broke up…"

"Have you seen the time?"

"I know, and once again I apologise, but I feel that I had to speak to you now because…"

"You ring me at gone midnight to complain about Mathieu having broken something in your bedroom, as if a 4 year-old would ever think of going upstairs in a stranger's house!"

"But I assure you…"

Too late. I wouldn't be heard. She'd put the phone down on me.

I wondered about the little boy, and hoped he didn't have too bad a night.

I would call back in the morning.

# A Time to Remember

A cold morning in January. We sit in the car, and wait.

"I told you we'd be too early," I gloat, "I said it wouldn't take more than ten minutes." I make the most of my superiority, as for once my knowledge of geography has proved more accurate than my consort's.

My husband shrugs his shoulders, trots out a "better early than late" rejoinder, and switches off the heating.

Of course, he's right, and bearing in mind the old saying that exactitude is *la politesse des rois* or the duty of kings - not that it did the French Royalty much good - it follows that as a Representative of the Republic - sorry about the kings - I should make it a *point d'honneur* of being on time.

Having to sit in an icy-cold car for half an hour and watch puddles turn solid is uncomfortable, and I try and think warm thoughts as I watch the world go by - somewhat underpopulated at this time of the morning.

Swinging tennis rackets and heavy sports bags, youngsters walk past, soon followed by large bottomed ladies in pink and purple tracksuits. A car pulls in next to ours, a middle-aged man, a grandpa no doubt, extricates a toddler out of a complicated harness, and carries her screaming towards the main building.

I glance once more at the invitation to attend ***The Opening of an Exhibition devoted to the Remembrance of Genocide and of the Holocaust***, to take place in the Sports Centre of a small Welsh town.

The location, almost industrial looking, strikes me as a strange place to hold such an event, but on second thoughts, I suppose there is no ideal place where to attempt to best convey to the young - and not so young - the horrors of those terrible events.

10.15. If we wait any longer I won't be able to move my legs. "Let's go in, shall we?"

My husband opens the car door. I cling to his arm - in my new black heels, balance qualifies as a challenge - and let myself be led through the double glass doors into an oasis of artificial palm trees whose branches bend and sway to a rhythm dictated by blasts of hot breeze from the gaping metal mouths of a full on air conditioning system. Our voices echo in the spacious hallway; we breathe in a mixture of disinfectant, wood polish, stale sweat, tiger balm, and I pick up a whiff of good old fashioned Germoline.

Now it's the chirruping of children's voices, a flock of them in their red and grey uniforms, hair shining, smiles on open faces, heavy shoes pounding the wooden floor, and we flatten ourselves against the wall to let them pass.

A woman hurries towards us. "Gwen, we spoke on the phone." Her handshake is firm. "Thank you so much for coming. No difficulty in finding us I trust?" She speaks with a gentle Welsh lilt.

"None whatsoever," offers my husband, "the directions you sent were easy to follow."

"Shall we proceed?"

We follow her as she sweeps down the long corridor in her ankle-skimming skirt, take a left turn, then a right and find ourselves in a large and well-proportioned room complete with fitted carpets and a rather elegant bar. "For evening functions," she explains, "the centre has to earn its keep." She nudges me forward. "Let me introduce you to the Mayor and his consort." Handshakes, the small talk *de rigueur* at such meetings, and as we are early she suggests the 5 of us take a look at the exhibition before I am due to formally open it.

We follow her once more as far as a door which she pushes open. It takes a few seconds for our eyes to get used to the semi-darkness. Our feet shuffle on bare boards, a violin sings its lament, and suddenly a siren screams an air raid warning. My husband cringes, draws back, holds his breath. We all do. None of us had expected to be shocked back to the past by the power of sound.

We step into the room and stand by a table laid with various artifacts: black bread, "baked by the local baker" our guide explains, before pointing to a small cardboard suitcase. "That was lent to us by a survivor of Ravensbruck. He will be coming to talk to the children about his life in the camp. He's a lovely man, a grandfather now and they'll be in safe hands." She surveys the room. "We feel it is important that history should come to life, become part of their heritage, whatever their religion or ethnic background."

We nod our approval.

"In the hope," she adds, "that as adults they can help prevent such atrocities happening again." She points to another table nearby. "Over there, the tresses were donated by a local hairdresser whose parents managed to get on one of the last flights out of Nazi Germany before the war was declared.

As Jews they more than likely would not have survived."

The visit continues. On to the games children played in the camps: snakes and ladders, with old buttons for counters, cards made of thin paper, a few toy cars and figures, clumsy shapes carved out of bits of wood, a skipping rope, a faceless rag doll.

A little further on, a row of 8 small wooden cups have been filled with lumps of fat topped with platted cotton wicks. I struggle to imagine men and women lighting the homemade candles and celebrating Chanukah - the festival of lights - in muted voices for fear they will be overheard and punished for wanting to keep their religion alive. I pick up a hollow bone, hold it up, and marvel at the crude copy of a Shofar, the traditional ram's horn blown at the New Year services and on Yom Kippur, the Day of Atonement.

More tables, more exhibits, more memories. Their power lives on in the ordinary, in their 3-dimensional reality, in the silence filled with sorrow.

When we think the exhibition is over there is more: we come face to face with blown up photographs of children, innocent victims of so-called ethnic cleansing, in Bosnia and Rwanda.

Starved, scarred, sometimes mutilated they stare at us and seem to be asking why?

"I think it's time we went back." Gwen's voice, despite keeping it just above whisper level, echoes in the silence lined with the sound of the weeping violin.

Back in the function room I shield my eyes from the sudden brightness of the lights, and struggle with the chatter and laughter of today's children.

"Better take our seats," suggests my husband.

We make our way to the front of the room. Faces – I find it hard to put a name to most of them – smile at us. A few handshakes. Words of little consequence. A wave here and there. The audience is larger than I had expected. Not far short of a hundred and fifty, not counting the thirty or so school children we saw earlier. They wriggle into a seating position on the carpeted floor at the foot of the platform enriched with a display of artificial daffodils, whisper to each other behind opened hands, and watch the audience we are to become file down towards our seats.

"Reserved" cards advertise our status. We are to sit in the front row next to the Mayor and other dignitaries. My husband helps me with my coat, and we settle as best we can on the unforgiving seats. The room is filling up. It won't be long before the beginning of the ceremony.

A gentle prod. He hands me a programme. A cursory glance at the front page. It is what I expected, a sheet of folded A4 with the date, venue and occasion clearly printed on the front page.

"Look inside."

I freeze. My tongue tries in vain to melt the icy smile burning my lips. I must have misread. It can't be. I stare. I blink. Look again. In bold print my name stares back at me. When the letters have done with dancing in front of my eyes they settle back and still spell my name. Now it's a surge of heat that threatens to engulf me. I don't understand. I did explain when asked if I would like to give the main speech that I would rather not, that sadly I hadn't been given enough notice to do justice to such an occasion.

My face is burning, and soon my brow and upper lip will need mopping. My hands hold on to each other for comfort.

"What am I going to do?" I whisper to my husband. He has the vacant look of a man taken over by events.

My instinct is to run away, far and fast, but I can't move.

A light tap on my shoulder. "You'd better take your place on the platform." Gwen nudges me forward, "the Mayor is about to say a few words."

My husband squeezes my hand. "Good luck."

It's a long walk to the steps, followed by a difficult climb. I catch my foot in the microphone wire, manage not to lose my balance, snag my tights on the leg of a chair but in full view of the audience I call upon my limited acting skills to help me look the very picture of confidence and respectability. I even manage a smile. Meanwhile my thoughts run riot: What shall I say? How to begin? And the ending? My head has turned merry-go-round. And it won't stop.

Hand clapping heralds the beginning of the proceedings. I force myself to breathe slowly through teeth welded in a fixed grin.

After the usual words of welcome from the chairman of the county, the Mayor takes his place in front of the microphone - set too high for me I notice - and I envy him the prompt cards he pulls out of his jacket pocket.

I have no idea how long he speaks for, and still no inkling of what I am going to say when my turn comes. My thoughts continue to spin out of control.

The applause tells me my turn has come.

I have no choice but to leave the relative safety of my chair, walk the few steps to the centre of the platform, and hope I find my voice.

"Ladies and gentlemen." I clear my throat. "Children…" I survey the fresh young faces turning towards me.

It's all about them, the future they can help create.

A slow intake of breath.

"Let me tell you the story of a child just like you. A Jewish boy who lived in Nazi Germany many years ago. Because they were Jews his parents were arrested and killed. He never saw them again. He managed to hide and escape, and later he was brought to Wales. All he could take with him were a few treasures he'd packed in a small cardboard suitcase just like the one you'll see in the exhibition. He showed me the case. He is an old man now but he remembers."

The children have grown very still.

Somehow words come to mind, ideas string together, my voice grows more confident, my stance more solid. Not that I can clearly remember what I said, but I treasure the memory of the few seconds' silence that followed my closing words, before the audience put their hands together.

# Lost and Found

*"Vous êtes le Consul honoraire?"*

*"Oui."* With the slap of the single word I hope to convey my displeasure at being disturbed early on a Sunday morning. That's one of the downsides of working from home, you can never ignore the phone.

"The office is closed, is it urgent?" If it is I shall have to deal with it.

"I'm not sure."

She'd know if it was an emergency.

"Can you please call back after nine on Monday?"

"It's about my daughters."

"If it's lost ID papers or applying for new passports, I'm afraid there is not much I can do on a Sunday."

"No, you don't understand. They've gone missing."

"What do you mean by missing?" Still in my dressing gown, I sit up to attention.

"I'm calling you from Corsica. I last saw Agnès and Dominique when they boarded their flight for London 10 days ago." I hear her gulp and blow her nose, before she resumes her story. "They promised they would…"

"How old are they?"

"Agnès is 20 and her sister has just turned 19."

Not children then, but it is alarming. They might be gullible enough to have got themselves in a difficult or even dangerous situation.

"Have you phoned the police?"

"I don't speak English, just a few words, not enough to be able to explain. In any case they wouldn't be interested, the girls are both adults." Her tone deepens. "I'm sure something has happened to them. It's not like them not to contact us, not like them at all. They know their father and I would worry."

I suggest that with the new university term about to start they might have been too busy looking for accommodation, registering for courses, finding their way, or maybe they had just lost their phone, possibly run out of credit. I do not point out that phoning parents does not usually figure on the list of essentials in a student's life, that the girls might just be suffering from a common attack of freedom rash.

I have failed to reassure my caller.

"Maybe they've had an accident and nobody has taken the trouble to let us know. Do you think we should fly over?"

"Let me see what I can do first. Had something bad happened I'm sure I would have been told." But would I? I will check with the Consulate in London just in case an accident has been reported directly to them and I'll give the local police a call. I refrain from sharing my thoughts with the anxious mother. "I take it you've contacted the university?"

"I did ask a friend to help but we never got through."

"What course are your daughters on?"

"It's a 6-month Erasmus exchange, and they are studying law. They've always been very good students." A shallow breath. "I'm worried sick."

I can imagine her, eyes puffed up with the crying, her handkerchief scrunched into a damp ball. "Leave it with me. Ring me back this evening. Hopefully I'll have some news for you." I jot down the girls' full names, dates of birth, brief physical descriptions and my caller's contact number.

Now to play detective. Law students tend to congregate in two or three halls of residence. I decide to try the one nearest town first, and if I don't strike lucky with any of them I shall have to contact the accommodation officer first thing on Monday in the hope I will be granted access to the lists of private addresses.

Early on a Sunday morning parking is easy, and the streets are almost deserted. Just the odd student about, hood up, ready to brave the October rain on a mission to get milk and other essentials, no doubt, after a heavy Saturday night.

The building complex is gated and I can't get in.

I press the caretaker's bell. The buzzer rings, but no voice enquires as to what I might need. There is only one thing for it; I shall have to tailgate someone going in. Not as easy as I'd thought; twice I try but get the look, the one that says 'what are you doing here? Go away'. Twice the door closes in my face. A change of tactic is called for.

My feet are soaking and my mood is deteriorating. Had I not committed myself to do my best to find the girls, I could drive home and spend the rest of the day by the fire with the Sunday papers and the cat for company.

"Excuse me."

The two young men I am addressing look surprised and stand by the gate, close to each other.

"I can't find anyone to let me in, but I need to, it's urgent." I pull my Consular card out of my wallet, present it for their scrutiny.

There is a moment of hesitation, they look at each other, speak a few words in Arabic, consult my official ID once more and with some reluctance they let me in.

Up and down staircases, along corridors. I put my ear to one door after the other - hope I don't get caught - and knock whenever I hear signs of life, unless the music is so loud I need to pound the door with my closed fist.

No luck. Either nobody answers or if they do it's to shrug their shoulders in ignorance when I ask about Agnès and Dominique.

Back in the hall downstairs I pin the sheet of A4 I printed before leaving the house asking in French and in English for the two sisters to contact me urgently.

I am on my way to another hall of residence when I spot two young women hurrying down the street. I look at them more closely: long dark hair, nicely cut jeans, smart leather jackets and a general air of elegance about them. They've been shopping in town.

They walk past me. I hurry back inside the enclosure behind them. The gate snaps shut.

*"Bonjour."*

They turn round.

*"Vous êtes françaises?"*

They huddle together under their sky blue umbrella, stare at me, nod a yes.

*"Agnès et Dominique?"*

"What do you want?" asks the tallest of the two sisters. The tone is almost aggressive.

Once again I produce my Consular ID card. "Your mother sent me." A lorry rumbles past us and I guess at their "oh" of surprise rather than hear it. When they fail to react I explain further. "She phoned me this morning, asked me to try and find you." For good measure I add that their parents are worried sick and why on earth have they not made any effort to contact them since their arrival in Cardiff?

"Well, we've been busy, you know…"

The mother takes over from the Honorary Consul: "No, I don't." I feel like picking them up by the scruff of the neck, like naughty kittens. Instead I march them to the nearest phone box, hand over some change, watch as they dial home, close the door on their conversation, and head back for my car.

# Chinon

Even when carefully expurgated for use in French schools, Rabelais never ranked as one of my favourite authors, so you can imagine my surprise when I was reacquainted with the bawdy 16th century writer - in a manner of speaking.

It all began with an invitation from the Welsh *bailliage,* or section, of the *Chevaliers Bretvins*, an order that does for Muscadet what the *Tastevins* do for Burgundy wine. We were to travel to Nantes, and spend a few days celebrating wine and food in the company of other *Chevaliers* from far and wide.

All of which sounded great, except that my capacity for both food and alcohol consumption is somewhat limited, and I was not sure how I would cope with an excess of both. Still, I rather fancied a few days in the old country, and was soon busy packing. Not a task to be undertaken lightly given the events listed in the programme booklet, and the Loire Atlantique weather which can prove as fickle as its Welsh cousin.

After an easy drive down to Plymouth, a convivial supper on board the ferry - we always start as we mean to go on - my companions were quick to point out, I managed a few hours' sleep before being woken up by a disembodied voice which filtered through the walls of the cabin.

"We are soon to reach Roscoff," it hissed. "Please make sure you have your belongings ready to disembark promptly." On the third replay I was out of my cabin, bag in hand, and climbing the steep stairs to the upper deck hoping a few deep gulps of sea air would clear my head.

As soon as breakfast was over it was time to get down to the cars, and we were on our way to Nantes, a town I had until now always associated with mourning clothes, silent funeral corteges and the strained conversations that followed the deaths of my paternal grandparents. It was many years since I had last put flowers on the family graves, and I was pleasantly surprised to find that the hotel where I would be staying was not only modern and comfortable but also at the heart of city, which would make a visit to the cemetery possible.

The next few days passed by in a whirlwind of official visits to sleepy villages and their welcoming *Maires*, leisurely lunches by the sea, an evening reception on the river Erdre, and dinners in fairy-tale castles. Helped by rivers of Muscadet they blurred into each other, and had me reach for

a bottle of mineral water as soon as I closed my
bedroom door.

By the fourth day I confided to one of the
*Chevaliers* that I could do with a different colour
wine.

"I know what you mean," he said. "It's
beginning to feel that way, but don't worry we'll
be in Chinon tomorrow evening and there'll be no
shortage of red. You'll see."

He wasn't joking.

The next day proved to be a scorcher, and we
were eager to climb on board the air- conditioned
coach which picked us up later that afternoon.

With their red collared gowns safely zipped
inside large plastic covers, their black hats and
white gloves respectfully carried by wives and
partners, the *Chevaliers* climbed on board the 40-
seater and we settled down for the 170 kilometre
journey to Chinon, one of Touraine's most
beautiful historical towns.

"Is it your first *Chapitre*?" asked Michel, the
*Chevalier's Ambassadeur* whom I knew from his
visits to Wales, as we neared the town.

"Yes," I told him, adding that I had no idea
what to expect.

"Well, it's unlike any other event you've
ever attended, especially a *Chapitre Solennel,*" he

grinned. "But I won't say too much or I might spoil it for you." A diplomatic answer which was possibly just as well in the light of what was to come.

As majestic as I remembered it, the fortress stood on a rocky promontory, still keeping watch over the town and the surrounding countryside. But now was not the time to concentrate on architecture and topography, and I turned my attention to the uneven stone steps and steep path that led us to a studded wooden door set in the rock at the foot of the castle. Here we re-grouped before being invited to follow the *Chevaliers* inside the cellar which, history has it, belonged to Rabelais' father way back in the 1500s.

To my surprise the first impression was one of space: high vaulted ceilings, spanning a vast chamber lit by bunches of upturned drinking glasses fitted with yellow bulbs. I noticed too the absence of mustiness usually associated with caves and cellars, and felt the light touch of an artificial breeze on my face.

I can't be sure how long I stood trying to make sense of my surroundings, but all at once the *Bretvins*, dutifully gloved, be-medalled, be-hatted, and dressed in their black robes, emerged from the *Robing* room. They proceeded along a wide

pathway lined with tall burning candles, and a row
of men attired in bright red robes edged with gold
and white fur, their heads crowned with the four
cornered flat red hats of their Order. Not a smile on
the faces of our hosts, the *Entonneurs
Rabelaisiens*, just a slight nod that barely suggested
recognition. I was puzzled at the change of mood
that had the guests now talking in low voices in
between sipping red Chinon wine, and nibbling at
dainty canapés.

It was a while before we were led up a series
of wide shallow steps, down a wide corridor and
into what I can best describe, with a nod to
Rabelais, as a gargantuan dining hall. By the time
the guests had taken their places, it would hold
close to three hundred people sitting at convivial
round tables of 10.

A hand waved at me. "This way, table
number 8!"

I elbowed my way through the noisy crowd,
to reach the group of *Bretvins* I was to sit with. Our
table was a few feet away from a short flight of
steps leading to the stage, but before I had a chance
to ask what it might be used for I was forced into
silence by the hush that descended on the
gathering. In a shimmer of golds and reds, the
*Entonneurs* processed through the dining hall, and

with studied dignity took their places at reserved tables.

There was the scraping of chairs on the stone floor and the guests resumed their conversations.

"What do you think of your first *Chapitre* so far?" asked Michel, the *Ambassadeur*.

"Very impressive," I managed to reply in between mouthfuls of melt in the mouth duck pâté. "You obviously have attended many of them."

"Yes, quite a few."

"Are they always that theatrical?"

"Yes they are, but this one is special, you wait until the *Entonneurs* welcome the new *Chevaliers*."

"What happens then?"

With his neighbour claiming his attention, and the rib of beef about to be served I didn't make sense of the reply, something to do with wine, of course. There was the hubbub of contented diners, the odd burst of laughter, the discreet sound of knives and forks on china plates, silent waiters clearing tables, and the meal was coming to an end.

Hardly had we began digging our spoons into the *crèmes brûlées* than a clear trumpet sound travelled through the dining hall. With measured steps, three trumpeters in blue and red medieval style tunics made their way towards the stage, soon to be followed by standard-bearers holding banners and flags that represented the different wine *confrèries* attending the gala dinner.

In a few well-choreographed steps and to the sound of the guests cheering and clapping, musicians and standard-bearers spread out before taking their position in front of the stage. It took a few seconds for the diners to settle, time for the *Entonneurs* to gather their robes and hats, push back their chairs and slowly climb the short flight of stairs. Looking rather formidable in their ceremonial garb, they proceeded to take their positions and stood, silent and very still behind the long narrow table, clad in golden velvet, that stretched from one end of the stage to the other.

"What's that about?" I whispered to my neighbour… or rather to an empty chair. I looked around and found him engaged in deep conversation with a stern looking man who just then glanced at me before nodding as if in approval.

I thought nothing of it.

Not, that is, until Michel returned to the table, where, after addressing a sort of general nod to the other *Chevaliers*, he leaned towards me to whisper.

"It wasn't easy but I've managed to get you in. You'll be going up with us."

"Going up where?"

He smiled but wouldn't say.

Had I known what was about to happen I would have put a hand to my head, complained of a sudden ailment, and pretended to choke - any excuse to leave the room - but naïve as I was I smiled back at him. Almost beamed when my turn came to climb the steps and join an assorted group of men, some I had never met before. Not that I trust my memory but the photographs I was to be sent later couldn't possibly lie.

As soon as the shuffling came to an end, the *Grand Maitre* of the *Entonneurs* took centre stage, cleared his throat, lifted his head, and waited for total silence.

"*Madame, Messieurs,*" an elegant nod as he briefly turned towards us, "you have been deemed worthy by your peers of entering the noble order of the *Entonneurs Rabelaisiens.* Before being put to the test and sworn as Chevaliers it is my duty to remind you that, as such, it will be your duty to advocate the humanist and gourmand views of Rabelais, our Master, and to promote the wine of Chinon wherever you go."

After a bout of lively clapping, the diners exchanged knowing glances, and shuffled in their seats to get a better look at the crowded stage, increasing my apprehension that the new *Chevaliers Entonneurs* were expected to do something.

But what?

It was not long before a light breath ran along the back of my neck, then what felt like a thin rope or possibly a ribbon rubbed against my skin.

What on earth…? A quick sideways glance at my companions, each one shadowed by an *Entonneur* busy tying large white bibs round our necks. Something to do with preventing us from making a mess of our clothing? Not that the deduction brought me any comfort. If anything it had my anxiety levels rising.

It reached a dangerous high when white gloved hands presented each one of us with a balloon wine glass the size of which I had never seen before, let alone held.

Helpless and mesmerised I stared at the hand that held the bottle in front of me as it hovered above my glass before tipping it slightly forward. I caught the deep gurgling of the wine, watched it flow and slosh against the sides, the level rising, higher still, until, in the hope that the red liquid might disappear if I wished it hard enough, I closed my eyes.

The wine was still there when I looked.

"Take a deep breath and drink in one go," said a disembodied voice.

My mouth turned dry, my right hand began to shake. I was losing my grip, and soon I would let go of the glass. It would shatter, the wine would spill, I would look a fool, and the now silent guests would burst into laughter. *You can't let that happen*, whispered a voice, my own this time, *and you are the only woman, you've got no choice*.

I must have raised my glass, put it to my lips, thrown my head back, and taken large gulps of the wine, again and again until the glass was empty.

I must have, but I can't remember. What I do recall is the gentle patting of a hand on my shoulder, the flash of cameras, hands clapping, a strange taste in my mouth, and wondering why I found it difficult to stand on the swaying stage.

"Steady!" This time the hand grabbed my arm. "Watch you don't fall as you go down the steps," said whoever was attached to the hand.

"What steps?" I asked, and what was that man in a funny gold dress talking about. I wanted to tell him I could fly anywhere I chose but a thick

63

tongue would not let me form the appropriate words.

"Just hold on to my arm," he said, and next thing I knew he'd dumped me on a chair, not too stable either, but giggling as I was, it no longer mattered.

No doubt the evening came to an end, someone helped me to the coach, carried me to bed, tucked me in, drew the curtains and let me sleep.

What do I care? I've got the bib, and the certificate, and Rabelais stares back at me from the medal dangling from its red and gold rope. All I am waiting for now is a chance to wear the insignia of my new status and boast of my achievement.

# A Geography Lesson

"Can you hold the line please? The Ambassador would like a word."

I dry my hands on the nearest tea towel, grab a pen and paper, and tighten the belt of my dressing gown, relieved I cannot be seen down the phone line. I do find Ambassadors intimidating and have to prevent myself from gushing down the phone to try and cover my nervousness.

A busy man, not one to spend long on the usual niceties, he soon comes to the point of his call. "As you know, the Pennal letter," (the name does not register) "is to be taken back to Wales and will be on show for a few weeks before being returned to France."

I nod in the direction of the cooker. "Yes indeed." I am not about to confess that this is news to me and that I have no idea what the Pennal letter is. Yet the tail end of an item on television brings to mind an article I saw in the press, something to do with Welsh history.

"My secretary will be contacting you in the next day or so to discuss the programme."

We say our goodbyes, very formal, very
French, and as soon as I've put the phone down I
rush to my computer to Google the Pennal letter.

The relevant sites are easy to find once I have
the spelling right – two '*n's* not one, and as I had
begun to suspect, it has to do with Owain Glyndwr,
a familiar figure in Welsh history; proclaimed
Prince of Wales in 1400 he had written to Charles
VI, King of France, to request help in his rebellion
against English rule.

The letter - which remained unanswered - has
its permanent home in the *Archives Nationales* but
would be on loan to Wales for a 6-month period.
Hence the need, as relayed by His Excellency, to
plan the handing over ceremony with the respect
due to such a document.

Two days later I am given my marching
orders by a secretary to the private secretary, and
told there will be a reception held in Cardiff for the
great and the good. I am to suggest venues and put
together an appropriate guest list; never easy as
there is always the danger of offending by
omission. Liaising with the person whose approval
I require is proving difficult. He is either busy, *en
rendezvous,* out of the office, *en déplacement*, or
just plain not available. He does not return my
calls, my faxes remain unanswered, and it is nearly

three weeks before he is available to speak to me, by which time I have booked a function room in a prominent hotel, sent out invitations, contacted the press, and done everything but ironed the flags. But I badly need clarification as to the timing of the 'temporary handover of the document.'

"I believe you wanted to speak to me?" There is definitely a note of condescension in my contact's voice.

"Well," I try sounding breezy and in control, "I want to make sure I have the timing right. If the official party is to be settled for a ceremony at 3pm, lunch has to end at 2.30 at the very latest. Would you agree?"

"I suppose so. You know Cardiff better than I do."

"Should they decide to walk rather than ride I shall of course have to inform the police so that they can provide adequate security."

"It's very simple." He detaches his words as if I am likely to have difficulty understanding him. "The Ambassador and his entourage will leave London mid-morning, and proceed to the venue for lunch, which should be over by two thirty or so. If they wish to make their way on foot rather than be driven to the National Library, half an hour will give them more than ample time."

I swallow hard. Grip the phone with my right hand. Take a deep breath. "Which library did you say?"

"The National Library." I imagine him raising his eyes towards the ceiling and sighing with impatience.

"The National Library. I see. Are you certain?"

"Of course. Surely you were told?"

'As a matter of fact whoever contacted me didn't specify. He referred to the library in Cardiff, which is why I wanted to speak with you."

"It stands to reason that the National Library will be in the capital. He used a different term, that's all."

"It's not that simple." I hesitate. "The National Museum is in Cardiff."

"That's what I mean, of course it is."

"But the National Library of Wales, I am afraid, is not."

"What do you mean?" The question sounds almost accusatory.

"It's in Aberystwyth."

"A Cardiff suburb, I take it?" He does not sound over concerned, while I know that short of using a fleet of helicopters, and where would we get them from, the visit will have to be revised. With only five days to go.

"No, nowhere near Cardiff." Silently I count up to ten, and still no reaction that I can hear, just voices in the background in the London office.

"How far?"

"2½ hours' drive at least, even with outriders."

When he speaks to me again it's to say that he will phone me back.

He never did.

# Misguided

The voice is strong, accented, the tone imperative. Possibly Scottish but I can't be sure. I switch on the loudspeaker as I am running late for my next appointment, and I need both hands to sort out my clothes, hair and makeup.

"I'm going to Paris in a couple of weeks' time," he bellows down the phone, "and I have a problem. You French don't make life easy."

I adjust the volume, turn it down one notch.

"How can I help?"

"I've consulted a travel guide but…" I hear him turn the pages, "I can't find the Orsay Museum."

"That's very strange." I pull a black skirt out of the wardrobe. "Are you sure?"

"Of course I'm sure. I want you to give me the address."

"I doubt that will be much help," I tell him, and suggest he looks up a map. "Find Le Louvre, that's on the right bank of the Seine, trace an imaginary path across the river and there you have it."

"The only map I've got is torn and, anyway, the museum should be in the guidebook."

I have to agree with him. "Don't worry you'll find it when you get there." A red jumper or a grey one? I can't decide, and one at a time I hold them against me as I face the bedroom mirror.

"That's not good enough. I am very particular when I go abroad. I don't like surprises."

I pull a funny face he can't see, bare my teeth, and fling the red jumper on the bed. The colour is too violent, I won't wear it today.

"But I promise you, it's there." I'm getting annoyed.

"Why isn't it in the book then, tell me that!"

"Look," I'm tempted to raise my voice but manage to repress the impulse, "it's really simple, the museum stands on the left bank of the Seine, not far from Le Louvre." I tap the palm of my hand with my hairbrush.

"If it's that simple tell me why is it that all I can find under Orsay is a railway station?"

"A railway station, you said?"

"Yes. I'd like to know what's that got to do with a museum?"

I think I do know. I open the chest of drawers and pull out a pair of tights, only to find that there's a big ladder running down one leg. Bother.

"Could you tell me the colour of your guidebook?"

"Whatever for?" His turn to sound annoyed, if not angry.

"Just tell me, if you don't mind."

"It's blue, of course."

"Of course. I see"

"I don't."

"One more thing, just to make sure. Could you please check how old it is?" He must have opened the guide because there is silence on the line, long enough for my face to contort in front of the mirror as I apply some lip gloss.

"It was published in 1983 by Ha… something. I bought it in a second-hand shop."

*You silly man.* I explain to him that the *Musée d'Orsay* was opened by President Mitterand in 1986, so of course it won't be listed in a Hachette edition dated three years before that.

"Why does it say station in the guidebook then?"

"Because it was built as a station in the late 1800s, and then transformed into an amazing museum."

"A station that became a museum? How on earth was I to know that?"

"Maybe buy a more recent guide in future, or look it up on the internet?"

But he's already put the phone down.

# When a Life is Taken

Street lamps flicker drops of yellow light on the roads, which are almost empty this early in the morning. When I get down town, the policeman on duty is warming his hands on a mug of coffee.

"Want one?" he asks. I thank him and gratefully receive his offering: the drink is hot and sweet, a bit on the strong side, just what I need before facing the cells. I have been here before but not often enough to get used to the sound of keys biting the metal locks open and closed.     Fresh from his early morning shower and shave, a young PC fills me in as we negotiate the last corridor.

"The accident occurred at about four this morning on a busy city road. Two vehicles involved in a head-on collision. The front passenger didn't make it. Died at the scene. The driver's name is Olivier."

"How is he?"

"I'm not sure he remembers what happened." He sighs. "High alcohol level when he was breathalysed. The doctor's been, just in case the lad sustained internal injuries. You can never tell with that kind of impact."

"And the others?"

"The odd scratch, a few bruises, but otherwise fine. They were lucky."

"Has he been allocated a solicitor?"

The police constable nods. "Yes, we've got one coming later. Nothing much will happen today, and we've got to respect the rest periods. You know how it is." He smiles.

I do. Only too well.

"Have the families been informed?"

"We asked our French colleagues to contact them both. Someone will be going to their homes. It's normal procedure." He unlocks a metal door, pushes it open and steps aside to let me in. "I told him you were coming."

I have seen rabbits caught in headlights, the way they stare without seeing, the frozen features, the near paralysis that roots them to the ground. Olivier has the look.

Lying on his back on the narrow bunk, head supported by what looks like a rolled up jumper, knees raised, feet resting on a dark green blanket, he stares at the wall facing him as if he were trying to decipher the messages carved into the plaster by others before him.

"Olivier?" I introduce myself. "I am here to check on your welfare. Is there anything you need?"

He groans.

"Are you in pain?"

He shakes his head, lifts it up. "They say I drove into an oncoming car and that Martin was killed."

"Don't you remember?"

"No." He buries his face in his hands. "We'd been to a couple of pubs, had a few drinks to celebrate the end of term. It was my car so I drove. We were all being silly, singing and laughing. Then someone screamed and it all went black." He catches his breath. "Is it true about Martin?"

"Yes, it is." That's all I can tell him. I reach out and rest a hand on his arm. "Is there anything I can do?"

We sit in silence for a while. "I'll come and see you later in the day if you like."

"Thank you." The words are blurred with tears.

-------------------------------

Impeccable in his navy police uniform, the family liaison officer appointed to the case suggests I might like a coffee while we wait at the motorway services.

"They are likely to be late." He tweaks the right cuff of his pale blue shirt. "With the amount of traffic on the roads and the state they are in, I hope they'll take their time and drive with care."

I dread meeting Martin's parents.

Try as I might, I can't think of words of comfort to offer them, and I keep wondering what I am doing here. Yet I cannot bear the thought of them driving straight to the hospital and having to struggle with the little English at their disposal when they reach the morgue, where no doubt they will be asked questions, and are likely to struggle with the formalities.

People pretend they don't notice the tall policeman by my side, but when he gets up, they shuffle to make way, avoid making eye contact, and the queue at the Wimpy counter waits in uneasy silence.

I have never liked motorway services, small artificial worlds encased in glass, plastic, and fake wood where the smell of fried onions, burgers and hot dogs, conflict with the sweetness of popping corn; the whole overlaid by the tang of cheap floor cleaning fluid. Not forgetting the false bonhomie of the holiday makers, the loneliness of the singletons lost in their thoughts or the headlines of a cheap daily while they munch on a chocolate muffin and sip at their latte.

Today, because we are in the middle of the festive season, a choir blasts out *We wish you a Merry Christmas* for the third time, and the fresh children's voices make me shiver. I can't reconcile their expression of joy with the loss of a son.

"Look," my companion juts his chin in the direction of a man and a woman dressed in sombre colours. They hesitate, scan the cafeteria, and shuffle forward. "I think it must be Martin's parents." The officer stands, tucks his hat under one arm and walks in the direction of the couple, crumpled in body and clothes.

It is not the first time I have been required to deal with a death, but never before have I had to come face to face with the bereaved mourning the death of their child.

We shake hands but our eyes don't meet. The four of us engage in the ritual of condolences, we offer, they receive. I am glad when it is over and PC Collins suggests we drive to the hospital 'to do the necessary'. He opens the car doors, and lets the parents in.

"I'll take you to your hotel afterwards. I thought it best to book you a room in town."

"And…" I step in quickly before they retreat in the dark depth of their thoughts, "if you'd rather not eat out in a restaurant my husband and I would be…" (I narrowly manage not to say delighted) "…would like to invite you to share a meal with us."

"*Merci.*" A tremor travels down to her hands folded in her lap.

"And we'll drive you back when you are ready, of course."

No flashing blue light. No need for speed. The police car moves slowly in the late afternoon traffic.

Night has fallen by the time we pull up outside the back entrance of the hospital, and I brace myself for the journey down the long corridors that run deep inside the building.

It is a small and silent cortege that processes along the shiny path clad with pale blue floor tiles. I am tempted to shield my eyes from the lights, so brash there is no room for shadows, but it would be indecent to show my small discomfort.

"Would you like to go and see him on your own?" asks PC Collins. He stands almost to attention outside the door of the morgue. "We'll wait here for you."

"Please..." Martin's mother reaches out for my hand. Her fingers are icy. I think of bloodless limbs, of her son's icy lips. "Please come with us I don't think we can face it on our own."

We step into the room, the four of us, and let the door close with a timid click. I welcome the gloom but feel disorientated by the absolute silence, the bareness of the walls,

There is nothing but the body of a young man stretched out on a trolley that stands in a kind of alcove at the far end of the room. He is almost smiling, and there are no signs of the fatal injuries he sustained at the time of the crash.

His mother calls out his name. And again, "Martin." The room swallows her sobbing. On either side of the recess two red curtains hang from the ceiling. I am reminded of a theatre performance, of the dead rising to take their bow at the end of a play. But here, the only movement comes from Martin's mother's lips as she prays before bending over to kiss her son's forehead for the very last time. She caresses his hair, runs her fingers over her child's face as if she wants to make sure never to forget it.

Throughout the final farewell his father has not moved. He does not cry. His breath is shallow, his fists clenched by his sides, his eyes half shut, and I wonder if he hopes that by refusing to look he might make the scene less real.

A gentle knock at the door. A young woman in medical whites and squeaky shoes steps in, offers her condolences and suggests we adjourn to the family sitting room.

"I'll get you some tea," she leads the way, "and you might want to sit down. Such a long journey." I am not sure which journey she refers to, the drive from Paris or the emotional trek that has just begun.

The tray may be cheap melamine but someone has taken the trouble to line it with a paper napkin. Chocolate biscuits on a small plate, and the tea is strong but drinkable. To begin with, apart from the chink of a metal spoon against the side of a cup there is silence, a veil of sorts, but not opaque enough that one can ignore the turmoil that hides behind. Little by little, sounds creep into the room: rushing footsteps down the corridor, a woman's laughter, a voice calling out. Martin's mother rummages inside her handbag, pulls out medicine bottles, shakes out a few tablets in the palm of her hand and gulps them down with a mouthful of cold tea.

"My heart," she explains, "faulty valve and quadruple bypass four years ago." She stares out of the window. "He was a good son." She smiles the mechanical lip-only smile of the bereft. "It has not been that easy for him all these years with me ill, but he was always kind and patient, pretended he was strong." Her hands rest in her lap. "We thought it would be good for him to study abroad for a year, give him more confidence." She moans like a wounded animal. "He sounded so happy the last time we spoke. He should have been with us for New Year, wanted us to meet his girlfriend, he was talking of getting engaged, making plans. And now…"

Her husband gets up, paces the room. "We were told there were four of them in the car…" he takes a couple of deep breaths, stares at a poster of a child on the wall facing him, "at the time of the crash."

PC Collins nods. "That's right. They'd been on a pub crawl. The accident happened in the early hours of the morning."

"I take it the driver was drunk?"

"They'd all had too much to drink."

"Don't make excuses for him, please. He committed a crime. He killed our son."

Martin's mother sags deeper in her chair. "He's the one who should have died, not our son, not my lovely boy."

81

I don't have the heart to tell her the driver walked away from the crash with no more than a couple of bruises. PC Collins remains silent.

It is 3 days since the fatal accident and Martin's parents have driven back to France, to their flat on the outskirts of Paris, to lives that have lost much of their contour and more of their purpose.

I have imagined them sitting on their son's bed in the room he shared with Simon, his younger brother, and wondered about his promotion from second to only son, about his new role, his reaction to the weight of his parents' hopes and fears for his safety, and how they'll cope if he makes choices they don't approve of.

------------------------------

The funeral director phoned earlier this morning. "The hospital will release the body at lunchtime. Would you be able to come over at about 3?"

"That will be fine."

"I believe you will represent the parents as we prepare the deceased according to French tradition?"

"Yes, they have asked me to stand in for them at the *Mise en Bière* and *Levée du corps.* I trust that won't cause you a problem?"

"Not at all."

Of all duties I have had to perform as Honorary Consul this one most certainly counts as the most upsetting.

For all my imagining I am not prepared for the men in the back room at the funeral home, for the white plastic aprons tightly wound round their assorted shapes, for the rumbling machine that blows air so cold I shiver in my winter suit.

"You may find this distressing," warns PC Collins, as he shuffles by my side. And I do.

It is almost with tenderness that the undertakers lift Martin from the trolley where he lay under a white sheet. As I step forward to watch over him the dead boy turns into a disorganised puppet. Obeying no master, his limbs flail by the side of his body, and I fear the men might drop him. I hide behind closed lids.

"Let me help." PC Collins pats me on the shoulder. "It won't be long now."

When I next open my eyes Martin is resting in a coffin lined with pale magnolia silk. Time for me to say the prayer his parents would have whispered to him as their final goodbye, to present him with the red rose his mother wants him to take to his grave, to cut a lock of hair she will carry in a silver locket round her neck. That last act I hesitate to perform, not that I fear touching the dead, find him repulsive or judge his mother's request to be unreasonable; it's the incongruity of my hand holding a small pair of scissors above the pale face of a young man I have only known in death that holds me back.

"I'll do it." The voice is steady, and once again I am grateful for the policeman who today gave of his own time to be by my side.

------------------------------

Back home, no sooner have I put the key in the lock that the phone summons me. A female police officer informs me that the parents of the young driver are on their way and would I meet them later today.

I will, I tell her, but not at the motorway services. I can't bear adding memories to my first encounter with Martin's parents. It will have to be at my home, the Consular Agency. She can explain where it is.

From the outset the meeting proves difficult. In view of the tragedy they are involved in - albeit unwittingly - I expect them to show concern for the parents of the victim, to express deeply felt regrets, to behave with the reserve befitting the occasion. Instead they reel out a few platitudes and almost raise their voices when demanding to know why their son has been arrested, and what, if anything, am I doing to secure his release?

That the blood test carried out shortly after the accident shows a high level of alcohol in Olivier's blood is not, in their eyes, sufficient ground for their son to be accused of a criminal offence.

The mother sits up in her chair, and tilts her chin back. "He drank a bit too much. That's what young men do. Surely everybody understands it was an accident?"

I point out that he was found to be six times over the limit and that his friend lost his life in the said accident.

"I don't know about a friend. I know he was on good terms with other students at university but I've never heard of a Martin. And anyway," she hisses, "you are supposed to be impartial."

The accusation is unfair but I let it go. She is overwrought. In time, I hope, she will see she is the lucky one, that unlike Martin's mother, her

85

anguish, her pain will end and that her son will be given back to her.

My offer of tea is brushed aside, and I struggle to think of something to say she will not find offensive.

"I was allowed to see Olivier in the cells, shortly after the collision," I tell both parents, "and I know how deeply sorry he is."

His mother bites her lower lip, her husband stares at the rose pattern on the carpet.

"I doubt very much he will be refused bail, so you should see him soon."

We say our goodbyes, and all there is left for me is to dread the prospect of a painful court case when the two families will come face to face.

# Thrown in at the Deep End

"Sorry to wake you but…"

I had mistaken the musical notes for birdsong but as my brain begins to stir I realise it's my new mobile.

"Hello, are you there?" I don't know the woman's voice but I recognise the French accent.

"I thought I'd better inform you that it is likely you'll be needed."

"Who's speaking please?"

There is an intake of breath. "There's been an accident."

"Are you the police?" With a daughter travelling in India I always feel uneasy when the phone rings outside what I consider to be normal calling hours, and judging by the light filtering through the thin curtains of the B&B where I am staying it can't be more than 5 o'clock.

"No, not the police. I am ringing from the Consulate."

"What's happened?" I was only appointed a couple of weeks ago and I'm not sure what's expected of me in an emergency.

"Tabarly has fallen overboard the Pen Duick and is feared drowned."

I switch on my bedside lamp - as if I can better understand with the light on - wriggle to the edge of the bed and let my legs dangle over the fake sheepskin.

"What did you say?"

"He was taking part in the Fife Regatta. It would appear he was struck by a gaff and fell overboard in heavy seas. His body has not been found."

"That's ridiculous."

Eric Tabarly, the father of French ocean sailing, the man whose passion has inflamed a whole nation and who managed to beat the Anglo Saxons at their own game. Tabarly. Drowned? It's as absurd as saying that the pyramids have taken to sailing down the Nile.

"We haven't been able to contact your colleague in Swansea, and it has been suggested I call you as you are the nearest to Haverfordwest."

I am spending the weekend in Bath, as it happens, but she doesn't need to know that.

"Hello, are you still there? You are the Honorary Consul, aren't you? I do have the right number?"

Of course she has. I've no idea who gave it to her, whoever she is, but I do think the joke is in very bad taste. I cut her off, not as satisfactory as slamming a proper phone down but right now it's the best I can do. Before dialling 1471 in case she forgot to block her number but the automated voice keeps repeating the caller withheld the number. She would.

Hardly have I had time to rest my phone on the bedside table that it lights up and warbles again. It's got to be her. I let it ring. I am not going to answer. I refuse to enter into this ridiculous game.

I lie back in bed, listen to the dawn chorus. Close my eyes. There's no point. I won't get back to sleep. 6 am. I pick up my book, read a few pages, put it down again, I can't concentrate.

I might as well get up, shower and dress.

It looks as if I am the first one down for breakfast. "Slept well?" asks the landlady.

"Yes, thank you." Not long enough, but I don't tell her that.

"Good, good." She busies herself with china, cutlery, jam (she refers to as preserve) and settles me at a small table by the window that overlooks the garden.

"Cooked or continental?"

I settle for orange juice, muesli and coffee. Better not eat too much I've got a birthday lunch to go to. On her way to the kitchen she switches on the TV secured to the wall over a defunct fireplace.

"In case you want to watch the news."

Which I don't but with the sound turned down the television is hardly invasive.

Until, that is, a familiar face appears on the small screen and grabs my attention. I gulp down a mouthful of tea to prevent myself from choking on the over toasted bread stuck in my throat, rush to the set, turn up the volume, stand statue still, watch and listen.

"There is growing anxiety over the disappearance of Eric Tabarly, the well-known French sailor often referred to as the `iron man`."

I struggle with the remote control and search for more information on other channels.

"Anything wrong?" asks my hostess who saunters into the breakfast room - she means with the breakfast I no longer have an appetite for.

I rush past her, run up the stairs, hurry into my room, look up the emergency number at the Consulate in London, tap in the digits. Get it wrong. Try again. I am too late. They did manage to contact my colleague, and as I pack I reflect that by refusing to believe the impossible I missed the opportunity to be one of the first to grieve over the loss of one of the most amazing of men.

# Let There Be Light

A couple of bills, an invitation to a charity dinner, and a reminder that my library card is about to expire. Nothing unusual about today's mail. The white envelope I pick up last looks innocuous enough. I slide the paper knife under the flap, pull out a single sheet of A4 folded in two, and have a quick look. It's an invoice from the Port Authority.

Odd. They usually phone if there is a small bill outstanding after the visit of a French Navy boat, so that I can inform the Attaché who then deals with the matter.

I am tempted to cast the payment request aside but the amount due, in bold at the bottom of the page, forces me to look more closely. I've no idea why a bill for `damages' to LP - whatever that means - should be sent to me. It has to be a mistake. I'll sort it out first thing in the morning. No point in phoning the Port Authority office this late in the afternoon, they'll be closed.

Meanwhile I have no intention of letting a payment request spoil the quiet evening I've been looking forward to. I drink a silent toast to the French Navy and the four training ships who spent the weekend in the Welsh capital, and are now sailing back to Brest.

It's a relief when such visits go well: no emergency to deal with this time, and both the lunch on board and the evening cocktail party proved a great success. I allow myself a second glass of wine, and decide on an early night.

Next morning the contact I want to speak to is at a meeting and, according to his secretary, likely to be tied up for the best part of the afternoon.

"Would you like to leave a message?"

"No, thank you I'd rather speak to him when he has a moment."

"I'll make sure he rings you back as soon as he's free."

It's gone 6 when he does call.

"Sorry it's been a heavy day. Have you recovered from your busy weekend yet?"

"Yes just about."

"Great evening last Friday by the way, I should have phoned to thank you, sorry."

"I was glad you could make it."

"What can I do for you?" Direct as always, he is a busy man.

"I received an invoice, obviously meant for someone else and I thought it best to have a word with you about it.

"An invoice? What for?"

"I have no idea."

"Can you read it out to me?"

I don't need to. I know the page contents by heart. "Repairs to LP: £775, followed by the usual request for prompt payment."

He chuckles. "Oh that!"

"Yes, that." Whatever that is.

"I'm sorry. Someone has been very efficient. I had no idea the letter had been sent out."

I am still in the dark.

"How can I possibly owe you such a large sum, and what does LP mean?"

"Well, the lamppost is badly damaged, it may even have to be replaced."

"The lamppost? What are you talking about?"

"Down in the bay."

Nothing to do with me I tell him, adding that I am not given to mad driving, and the last time I collided with a streetlight was in a Bristol car park, many years ago.

"I didn't say you were responsible."

"Didn't you?"

"Of course not but I originally thought that as the HC you'd be the best person to send the invoice to."

"I don't follow, sorry."

"To tell you the truth I am not quite sure how it happened, but it would appear that after casting off, the last of the training ships got too close to the side and caught one of our brand new lampposts."

"I see." I can well imagine the scene, the embarrassment, and the red face of the culprit.

"We've had it looked at and it will need to be repaired, or even replaced. Don't know yet. In any case…" He hesitates.

"Yes?" Now is not the time to leave me in suspense.

"On second thoughts I asked for the invoice to be withdrawn, which obviously it was not. I suggest you simply ignore it. We can't risk a diplomatic incident, can we?"

"Certainly not." I try my best to match the humorous tone of his voice. "That would never do."

"Good, that's settled then."

"Thank you, that's very generous of you."

All the same, I was tempted to point out that planting lampposts so close to the edge of the

94

water put them at risk of becoming the unfortunate victims of a trainee naval officer. I thought better of it, and kept quiet. It wouldn't do to appear ungrateful.

# A Matter of Convenience

Toilets? Did he say *toilets*?

The line's gone dead. The voice of the Commanding Officer has drowned somewhere in the middle of the Atlantic Ocean, together with any chance of asking if I'd heard him correctly.

Why would he say *toilets*? I must have misheard, my sensible self tells me.

But then, maybe I didn't. Too late now. I nudge the thought away. I need to concentrate on the ship's visit confirmed by the staff of the London Naval Attaché late last night.

I bring up the email, read it again, open the attachment, and have a good look at the photograph of the ship expected to reach Cardiff the weekend after next. Fat-bellied, painted white, the 21 metre long cutter with its single engine doesn't fit into any of the categories of French Navy ships I have become familiar with over the years. As for her living quarters, it's hard to believe they can hold a crew of up to 18.

Which explains why there will be no formal lunch on board, and only a limited number of guests at the evening cocktail to be held on deck.

It follows that high heels are ill-advised, and I make a mental note to further advise the ladies they might like to bring jackets or warm scarves. Even in June a cold breeze is likely to blow across Cardiff Bay.

I return to the notes I was sent, wondering why the name of the ship sounds familiar.

I am pretty sure my father, a keen sailor, mentioned her to me, something to do with the war, I recall, and exceptional circumstances.

I run a finger down the next few lines and, yes, of course: Le Mutin, it's all there.

With a growing sense of excitement I read all about the ordinary French training ship which turned spy when she joined the British Navy during the second world war; how, disguised as a fishing boat, complete with fake tunas - courtesy of the British Museum - stuffed with explosives, she engaged on infiltration missions, before being returned to the French Navy and her role as a training ship at the end of the war.

Intrigued, I look forward to greeting Le Mutin, now in her 83rd year, as soon as she reaches Cardiff.

Not long now; I'd better get busy with the extensive list of arrangements to be finalised: fill in the request for the usual courtesy visit to the Lord

Mayor, put the last touches to the guest list for the reception, email the invitations, ensure I've been given the right ETA, contact the Port Authority, check on the berth facilities - waste collection, water and electricity supplies, not forgetting the Ship Chandler who deals with the food supplies, and, most importantly, the mobile phones.

A few minutes to update the mini Cardiff Guide I've put together - minus the cycling trails this time as I can't imagine the crew stowing folding bikes on board - and I email the attachment to the ship.

I lean back in my chair. Straighten up. I nearly forgot about the hull inspection. Must tell the ship where to go to obtain the permission to dive.

I should feel relieved the preparations are in hand, but as always with the planning of a ship's visit there is the little voice reminding me that at the last minute I may have to deal with a cancellation; more frequent in the winter months, nothing one can do about angry seas, and there is always the possibility of a ship being requested to change direction and attend in some faraway part of the world in case of conflict.

D-Day minus 2. All is well, it looks as if Le Mutin is on her way to Cardiff.

"Phone!" calls my daughter as I am on my way to drive the "official vehicle" - aka my husband's car - to be washed and polished.

"Any progress with the toilets and the showers?" asks a voice I cannot identify.

"Who's speaking?"

The name means nothing but the tone is military enough for me to guess the man is sitting close to the Naval Attaché's desk, and in any case, no one I know would be quizzing me about how far I got securing the use of toilets. That dreaded word again.

"Pardon?"

"I believe you were asked."

"Actually…"

"After weeks at sea the crew is looking forward to some comfort and the use of proper facilities."

"The thing is…"

"Surely you know about the restrictions on board Le Mutin?"

My mind goes back to what I read about the tight sleeping accommodation in the drawer-like bunks. But no toilets? How do they manage when they are at sea? Best not to argue. "I'll do my best," I tell him, with no idea of what I mean by that.

"By the way we've got two women on board - and if you are thinking in terms of hotel rooms, remember we've got a tight budget."

A nice parting shot.

As soon as I've put the phone down I get busy with my address book. Short of a number for an emergency plumber, I have no connections in the world of public conveniences. I start dialling: friends, colleagues, acquaintances. I get nowhere. Time to drive down to the docks and have a word with the Seafarers Mission.

"Sorry," they tell me, "we'd like to help but we've only got the one loo and the shower is pretty basic." Still, they would love to welcome the French crew and share a drink with them.

Irritation reaches a peak when I am told that, had I known sooner about these wretched toilets, the County Hall - a stone's throw away from the dock where Le Mutin will be moored, might have been able to help. It's too late now to deal with the necessary paperwork.

"What a shame," sighs the lady I speak to.

It will have to be hotels.

The ones in the bay are full to bursting.

"It's the motorbike race," I'm told, again and again, "you'll be lucky to find a room in the city this weekend."

Find one I do, but I go from elated to deflated in the space of a few seconds when I am told the price - so extortionate I can't even begin to consider booking it.

It's past 9 o'clock, and still nothing. My husband is less than enthusiastic when I suggest that perhaps we should offer the use of our spare room to the 2 lady crew members. I'm not keen either, but I have no idea what else to do.

I am on my way to bed when my mobile rings its happy tune. I am tempted to ignore, but it might be an emergency. I recognise the young voice of the receptionist from the Travelodge. "Are you still looking for accommodation?" she asks.

"Yes, of course." I hold my breath.

"We've had just had a room cancellation. You want it?"

The price seems fair, barely more than what they charge on an ordinary weekend.

"Yes, yes. Great." It's not that great really, but at least I will have something to present the CO with tomorrow.

Morning sees me standing side by side with the Liaison Officer from HMS Cambria. The team from the Port Authority is already in place, and together we watch Le Mutin make her entrance into the Roath Basin, at a slow and dignified pace as befits the most senior ship of the French Navy.

As soon as the gangway is in place we step on board. The CO greets us with the offer of the traditional cup of coffee which, he indicates, will be served below deck. We climb down a short ladder and straight into the mess room, where we take our places on the benches round the table, just large enough to accommodate the crew at meal times.

"Compact, isn't?" The second in command points to the narrow bunks. "With *bannettes* that size they certainly have to learn to keep tidy. Better too if they don't snore or suffer from seasickness!"

"Sailors get seasick?" I ask.

"They certainly do."

In such close quarters…. the very thought makes me feel queasy.

"But we manage, and the lack of privacy doesn't seem to put people off. We get oversubscribed every year. Let me show you round," he grins, "not that there is that much to see."

He slides a narrow door open. "The Pasha's quarters." I hide a smile at the CO's nickname I know to be inspired by the Ottoman Empire.

"Pretty basic as you can see... and he has to share with the Quartermaster."

A few steps and we've reached the galley. The Second describes it as compact. I'd say narrow and very small.

"It's been recently refurbished." And he points out the new stainless steel sink, the two freezers and the laminate surfaces. "Pure luxury." I think he means it.

Hard to think of any space left for toilets and showers anywhere on the ship, and my unease turns to deep embarrassment when he pushes a door open and stands aside for me to look into . . . a diminutive loo, and shower to match.

"No hope of improving on those, but better than in the old days, when they had to make do with direct access to the sea... if you see what I mean." He is enjoying my confusion. "I'll show you when we get back on deck. Talking of toilets, did you...?"

We are back in the mess and I am about to admit to my failure at finding appropriate facilities when the Liaison Officer butts in.

"What if we drove you all to HMS Cambria tomorrow morning, and show you what a proper Welsh breakfast is like, and give you a chance to clean up?"

I could hug him.

"Where is she moored?" asks the CO.

"*She* is a set of buildings in Sully on the outskirts of Cardiff."

The suggestion has gone down well, but I still have to share my news.

The CO turns to me. "We were rather hoping…"

"I know, and I am really sorry but there's been something of a breakdown in communication. I didn't know about your needs and request until yesterday, and Cardiff is full to bursting with a motorbike race, so I'm afraid…"

He nods. Being at sea on Le Mutin must encourage a certain type of stoicism, because when we meet later that evening, he shows no signs of annoyance and proves a perfect host, happy to entertain his guests with seafaring tales.

When the time comes to disembark, the CO calls me over.

"I think we'll give the girls the hotel room. They'll appreciate hot water and a couple of nights' privacy."

"Fine, I'll collect them tomorrow late afternoon and take them to the Travelodge. How will the others manage?"

"We'll find a way, don't worry."

I tried not to.

Next morning, the bulk of the crew - some have to stay on board - pile into the Royal Navy minibus, and are soon on their way to the base to Hayes Point, the home of HMS Cambria, while I turn my attention to a young sailor in urgent need of a dentist. Then it's time to collect the women officers and drop them at their hotel where they plan on wallowing in the bath, ordering pizzas and watching television from the comfort of proper beds.

Tempting.

Sunday; the sun shines over the capital, the ship's visit is going well, and I am looking forward to the day ahead.

Until the phone call.

"Excuse me, I'd like to speak to the…" the usual mix of council, councillor, counsellor but I know they mean me.

"Yes?"

"The manager would like a word."

"Something wrong with the payment?" That's all I can think of.

"I can't say, sorry, he would rather tell you in person."

"I'll hang on."

"Sorry, I mean, he'd like to see you."

"See me?" I don't fancy driving down to the bay. "Is that absolutely necessary?"

"I believe so, yes."

All very mysterious.

Twenty minutes later, Stephanie - so it says on her badge - is waiting for me at reception.

"If you'd like to follow me please." I trail her down a narrow corridor, until we reach a door marked 'Private'. She knocks.

"Enter," shouts a man's voice.

He is younger that I had expected, late 20s, and ill at ease, judging by the twisted paper clips lying on his desk.

"Come in please." He stands up. "Do sit down." He points to the small leather armchair facing him, clears his throat, says nothing.

"You wanted to see me?"

"It's a rather delicate matter."

Delicate? I have no idea what he is on about.

"It's about the 2 young French women you booked in last night."

"Yes, and I did ask if there'd been a problem with the payments."

"No, nothing to do with that. The thing is…" he is staring at his feet, "I'm not quite sure how to put it." I wish he'd get to the point. "It's . . . rather embarrassing. You see -"

I don't.

"It has come to the attention of my staff that the two young ladies in room 28 have had - are having -" he is flustered, his cheeks turn a baby pink, "a large number of visitors, male visitors, that is, and -"

"Oh I know," I tell him.

His cheeks flare up. A sharp intake of breath. He is struggling for words. "You know?"

"Yes I do, and I am really sorry. I did mean to ask you if you'd mind."

"Mind?" He sits down, wriggles in his chair for a while, slowly raises his head and does his best to look at me. "We pride ourselves on running a family establishment and I am surprised you would even ask me if I'd. . ." his words tumble over each other, "allow men, a succession of men to…"

"16 of them, I believe." I am beginning to enjoy myself.

He stares at me open-mouthed.

"I suggested it."

"You suggested it?" His mouth opens a little wider.

"Yes I did, because there is one toilet on board, you see, and only one shower for emergencies, as it were, and when they've been at sea for days on end, all they want…"

Poor man, I've lost him.

"… is a hot shower…" I can almost hear the little cogs in his head trying to make sense of this deluge of information, "… as you can well imagine."

Looking at him gawping back at me, I am not sure he is imagining the right thing.

"Let me get this right." He screws his eyes tight, throws the now useless paperclips in the bin by the side of his desk.

"Didn't I say?" I raise my eyebrows in innocence. "The 2 young women are naval officers and the men you are referring to are colleagues from the same cramped ship, and all they were after was the use of the bathroom. Nothing more, I assure you."

His expression turns blank. He has no words available, it seems, and like those toy dogs who sit on the back ledge of cars all he can do is nod his head.

"I trust that closes the matter satisfactorily."

I shut the door quietly behind me and walk away.

# Caught Out

Like most people I have an ambivalent relationship
with my phone: in turn I love it, hate it, curse it,
but I don't suppose for one minute that I could live
without it. I only wish it would flash a warning
light when the caller is on the war path, just to give
me time to prepare myself.

On that Monday morning the barking voice
took me by surprise.

"*Consulat de France?*"

"*Oui, ici l'Agence consulaire.* Can I help
you?" I sound like a well-trained receptionist.

Few people jump straight into the "let's be
rude she's only a civil servant" mode, but the man
at the other end of the phone doesn't even wait to
draw breath.

"You've got me in a right bloody mess!"

I am almost sure I heard a fist thumping the
hard surface of a table or desk.

"I beg your pardon?"

"I've never met with such incompetence!"

I have no doubt as to my ability to make
mistakes - only those who never strive to achieve
get it right all the time - but have no idea as to the
cause of his accusation.

"Could you explain how I can help?" I resist the desire to add that a little civility would not come amiss.

"I am due to get married next month in Limoges…"

"How nice…"

"But now I've been told I can't because some idiot forgot to register my divorce."

"I see." I drag a chair and get myself ready for the rest of the tale, because of course there is more to come.

"No, you don't. How the hell do you expect me to tell my wife-to-be that our marriage will have to be postponed?"

"Do I take it that both your first marriage and divorce took place in Wales, and that there is no mention of the latter in the margin of your birth certificate?"

"You bet there isn't, and all that because you didn't do your job properly."

At this stage, to tell him that it may take months before he can actually tie the knot a second time, in France at least, does not seem a good idea. Too much like waving a rag, red or otherwise, in front of the proverbial bull.

Instead, I suggest that as long as he in possession of the decree nisi and the decree absolute the marriage could take place anywhere in Britain.

"You must be joking!" he shouts all the way from the old country. "That's out of the question."

I change tack. "When did you ask for your decree absolute to be registered?"

"In Cardiff. 18 years ago." His tone oozes confidence.

"Are you sure?"

"Of course I'm bloody sure. I went to the consulate in Queen Street, handed over all the necessary documents and was told it would take a few weeks, months maybe, but not years for the divorce to be registered in France."

"You mean in 1988?" I doubt he would appreciate the Cheshire cat expression on my face as my eyes run over the framed lists of career Consuls - some very un-republican, including a Duke and a couple of Counts with very long names - a reminder the long French presence in the Welsh capital.

"Yes, I've already told you."

"There is obviously a bit of a problem here…"

"You're telling me. And what are you going to do about it?"

I measure my words, roll them in my mouth before setting them free: "There is a problem, because… you see... there no longer was a French consulate in Cardiff in 1988. It closed in 1984."

Silence. And a few seconds later the buzzing of a free phone line.

I never heard from my caller again.

# Prisoners

"Come as soon as you can." My husband had
scribbled the message and an address on the back
of a used enveloped, and propped it up against the
still-warm kettle.

I dropped my bag on a chair, and sighed. All
I wanted after a long plane journey was a long soak
in the bath, an hour's mindless television and an
early night. No chance.

Dusk was falling when I pulled up outside
the house. Number 56 was in need of a coat of
paint; the windows grimy and the bell did not
work, but there was nothing on the outside to
indicate anything was amiss in the ordinary
looking semi that stood on the corner of the
treeless street.

Hardly had I knocked on the door than I
heard a key turning in the lock. Still in his work
suit my husband let me in, motioned me down a
narrow corridor towards a dark kitchen, put a
finger to his lips the way children do when silence
is part of their game, and closed the door behind
him.

"Keep your voice down, I think she is
sleeping." He leaned back against the sink half-

filled with dirty dishes, took off his glasses, and pinched the bridge of his nose.

"What's going on?" I cleared a pile of clothes from a chair, sat down, taking in the pink and purple paint splashes on the walls, the scratched lino, and the air of neglect everywhere I looked.

"I had a call, or rather you did, from the police. Apparently there has been a disturbance. It would seem that Juliette," he dropped his voice, jutted his chin in the direction of an upstairs room, "had a go at some woman collecting for a charity. The girl went for her, gave her a black eye and frightened the life out of the poor thing."

"Why involve me? What about the police? I'm not sure I understand what this has to do with me."

"Well, Juliette is French…"

"Yes, I gathered that."

"…on some university exchange scheme, and renting a room in this place," he let out a sigh, "with a Mrs Morgan, who happens to be away for the weekend, not due back until late Monday evening."

"And I suppose that landing a punch in someone's face does not qualify as serious enough for the girl to be arrested, but they want me to keep an eye nonetheless?" I opened a cupboard door in search of teabags, found a few loose ones next to a sticky ketchup bottle.

"Exactly." He ran cold water in the sink and filled up the battered old kettle. "The police managed to get through to the mother with the help of an interpreter, and it would seem Juliette had some psychiatric problems before coming here."

"Don't tell me," I hunted for the sugar on the sticky shelves, "I'm going to be stuck here with a disturbed young woman I've never seen before, until social services can get their act together."

He nodded. "Got it in one. *We* are stuck with it." He ran his finger along the rim of a thick mug and handed it over to me. "No chips. Looks safe enough."

The tea tasted as I imagined hot stewed paper would. Anthony made a face, took a few sips, paced the room. Suddenly he held up his free hand.

"Listen."

I looked up.

"I think I can hear her moving about in her room." He opened the kitchen door and turned to me. "You'd better come too."

I plodded up the stairs after him, and we reached the landing, home to discarded toys, lone shoes and cardboard boxes filled to overflowing.

"What exactly are we supposed to do with her?" I whispered.

"Keep the peace, make sure she does not leave the house, and wait for the medical team to come and assess how bad she is."

"On a Friday night? Pretty unlikely I'd say. I can't see anyone rushing to see her." I picked up a broken doll and settled it on the window ledge next to a headless teddy bear.

"How can anyone live in such a mess?" I shrunk away from bright red, damp-smelling towels draped over the banister. "Did Juliette's mother say what was wrong with the girl?"

"No. All she kept saying is that Juliette may have been disturbed but has never shown signs of violence before. She fears she might try and harm herself."

He pointed to a closed door, tapped on it gently. "Juliette, are you alright? Would you like to come down and have something to eat or drink?"

"Is that wise?" I kept my voice low. "Isn't it best to leave her where she is?"

He shook his head. "The window worries me. What if she tries jumping out?"

This time he knocked on the door, and drew me forward. "You speak to her; she might be frightened by a man's voice."

We changed places. "Juliette…" I hesitated, pressed my forehead against the door, raised my voice a little. "We haven't met but I think it would be nice if we had a chat. Why don't you come out?"

Footsteps, the sound of a piece of furniture being dragged on bare boards, followed by what I took to be a sob, that turned to some sort of laughter and back again.

"Juliette," I pleaded, "let me in. I won't stay if you don't want me to, I promise."

"It's hopeless," said my husband.

I crouched on the floor, rested my back against the wall. "Let's wait a little longer."

When Juliette did open the door I forced myself to stay very still.

She smelt of unmade beds, her long black skirt had gone grey with wear and too many washes, and only later did I notice she was pretty, or would have been, had she brushed her greasy blonde hair away from her face.

"Who are you?" she asked. "What are you doing here?"

I stood up and let Anthony introduce us. "We are friends of Mrs Morgan's," he explained. "We've come to keep you company for a while."

117

Juliette frowned, bit her upper lip, lowered her head, and looked at us sideways on.

"You would call her by her first name if you were her friends." She made to push me away with her hand. "I don't want you here." I stepped back, and waited.

From dark to light her mood changed, like throwing a switch.

She spoke our names aloud, as if to try and convince herself she had heard them before, shook her head from side to side and smiled.

She followed us to the kitchen. The only fresh food I could find was half a dozen eggs. I scrambled a couple, and offered her a few spoonfuls on a slice of stale toast. She picked at it, chewed slowly, pushed the plate back, and wiped her mouth with the back of her hand. She accepted the mug of tea with some reluctance, only to pour it down the sink a few seconds later.

"It's been poisoned, someone wants to kill me."

I suggested we might be more comfortable in the front room, but Juliette would not move from the battered old armchair in which she sat, hunched up on herself like a forgotten rag doll.

"Don't!" she shouted when I reached out to switch on the television. She thumped the side of

118

the armchair with bunched fists. "You mustn't touch it, it's plugged into the Secret Service and they are looking for me. I know they are." She got up, covered the set with a tea towel. "Nobody can see us now."

"But…" I said.

My husband's stare warned me not to argue. "What about the radio?" I asked.

"Just as dangerous. The voices pretend to be human, and the music is coded, it forces you to do things, bad things against your will."

I looked at my watch. It was going to be a long night.

By 10 o'clock we had lost all hope of being rescued by the medical services. Juliette remained crumpled up in a corner of the settee, chewed the inside of her cheeks, and muttered to herself. For reasons only she could understand she sprang to her feet, paced the room, hopped over a stain on the rug and rushed out into the corridor.

"Don't come near me," she shouted, "go away!"

She moaned and screamed. Then came the wailing and the fist thumping. Later we watched as she tore her nails in an attempt to climb the walls, like some trapped Kafkaesque creature. She collapsed, sobbing, on the tiled floor, and it took all

119

of the strength we had left to drag her back to the relative warmth of the kitchen.

Throughout the night she wove an irregular pattern of frenzied activity and near catatonia. She'd rush up to the first floor, look for dark places, and run back down again to hide under the stairs, "to be with those who understand me" she screamed at us, when we tried to hold her back.

Morning found me stretched out next to my charge on the dirty mattress of an unmade bed. I listened to her regular gentle breathing, eased my body away from hers, and watched her sleep. I barely recognised the Juliette of the night in the face softened by an almost babyish smile. The mother in me was tempted to caress her cheek as I would my own child, but I refrained, for fear of breaking the spell and robbing her of the peace which, I knew, would take flight as soon as she woke.

The morning dragged on.

Unwilling prisoners of the girl entrusted to our care, we welcomed street sounds: cars driving past, children laughing, women chatting as they walked by the downstairs windows. We took it in turns to watch over Juliette while we showered and dressed in yesterday's clothes. We tried to entice her to freshen up, but she refused, would not let us near her, remained curled up in the old armchair, and we let her be.

It was mid-afternoon by the time the medical team came to our rescue. They introduced themselves: a young general practitioner, a social worker, and a middle-aged psychiatrist. The three men wore solemn faces, in contrast with their weekend garb: faded jeans, baggy cords, scuffed sneakers, and open neck shirts.

I busied myself with tea bags and instant coffee. My husband poured the milk, stirred in the sugar, handed over the mugs. We could have asked to be released, but after spending the night looking after Juliette it felt wrong leaving her with strangers whose presence she was bound to find threatening.

She didn't seem to mind. Not at first. She kept humming a lullaby, and drawing shapes with an index finger she dipped in the cocoa tin.

As soon as I suggested we might be more comfortable in the living room, Juliette's face reverted to its frightened look. She was the last one to sit down, in an armchair fitted with loose covers, that she picked at with her broken nails, until she turned a small tear into a gash that revealed blue corduroy. She blinked a few times, seemed surprised at what she had uncovered. "There,

121

there," she kept saying, and patted the chair as if she wanted to make it better.

She kept glancing at the three who would decide on her immediate fate, then quickly closed her eyes as if she couldn't bear to look at them.

At last they had reached an agreement. The social worker got up and reached out for Juliette's hand. Quickly withdrawn.

"Keep away from me. The devil sent you. I know."

The young man moved back. "Juliette, you are not well, and we think it best for you to spend a few days in hospital so that we can make you better."

She sprang up from the armchair and made for the door.

"Don't go!" I called to her.

"If you put me away I'll die, I know I will."

"No you won't and nobody will hurt you, I promise." She let me stroke her arm before crossing both of them over her chest.

"I'm not going. I want to stay here. With you."

It struck me as ironic that now we wanted her out of the house she was prepared to fight us for the right to stay put. And fight she did, with her fists, her legs, her elbows. Then came the

122

screaming, the dry sobbing, and when she was spent she let herself slide down to the floor.

I knelt by her side. "Would you like me to come with you?" The words surprised me as much as they did her. My husband shook his head, reached out for my hand and squeezed it hard.

Juliette let out a moan.

"And I'll come and visit you every day if you like." I stroked her hair, her cheek, put an arm round her shoulders, helped her to her feet, and together we began the slow walk to the ambulance that was to take her to the locked ward of the red brick psychiatric hospital where corridors echo with the voices of lost minds.

# Goodbye, not *Au revoir*

"There you are..." The undertaker grabs my wet umbrella, and pops it into a tall china vase by the side of the door. Accustomed as he must be at dealing with the dead, for whom time no longer has any meaning, I find the way he keeps glancing at his watch rather irritating.

"We did say 10.30," I remind him, and as if to oblige, a clock strikes the half hour in a mournful way.

"Yes, of course, of course." The handshake is business-like; it goes well with the dark grey suit, the sparkling white shirt, and the regulatory black tie. The message is clear. Here stands a man you can trust; the only discordant note in his appearance, the mop of red hair which he has tried, and failed, to tame, despite a heavy handed dose of hair gel. "Let's go into my office, shall we?"

I follow him down the thickly carpeted corridor.

"Do come in." He ushers me into a long and narrow room which hides the lack of windows with the help of large gilt framed pictures: one of a lake, a translation of serenity, complete with muted orange sun about to drop off the horizon, while the other offers wispy clouds brushed lightly onto a clear blue sky. They hang in recesses dressed with pelmets and pink curtains on either side, windows looking nowhere.

Mr Evans invites me to sit in a comfortable armchair, while he takes his place behind the mahogany desk, as would a captain of industry. A little hand rubbing, a pull at his jacket sleeves, a thin smile in my direction and he tells me that he is concerned about the deceased.

"Concerned?" I ask.

"He's not looking himself."

"In what way? I am tempted to point out that three days into eternal life, the French citizen whose remains I have come to help dispatch back to the country of his birth, is entitled to have disassembled a little from his alive self. However I refrain from such a comment for fear of sounding flippant. "I'm not sure I quite understand what you mean?"

"If you'd like to follow me to the Chapel of Rest you'll see for yourself."

By the time we reach the wood panelled room an assistant has joined us, a middle-aged woman, efficient looking despite the handkerchief she holds in her hand, ready to stem the effects of a bad cold.

125

There is the smell of synthetic lavender from the plug-ins placed strategically on either side of the cheap coffin, the handles too bright to be silver.

"Look at him."

I lean over the coffin, lined with cream silk for a touch of lasting comfort and elegance, and through a glass panel cut out of the pine lid I stare at a man's face, almost comical because of the beret at a slant on his head, in cheeky contrast with the hands folded neatly across the chest where the rice-shaped beads of a rosary drip red on the white shirt.

"Cirrhosis of the liver," whispers my companion, to explain the yellow tinge of the dead man's skin. "He's not as old as he looks." He sighs. "And I gather he lost a lot of weight in the last few weeks of his life, but still…"

He hands me a tattered passport and yes, he's right, the photograph curling with age at the corners looks like that of a latter day Elvis: the thick neck of a fat man, eyes shrunk under puffy eyelids, bloated cheeks, unsmiling lips, and dark hair in such abundance it might belong to a toupee.

"I see what you mean." Which is no help when it comes to trying to decide whether to proceed with the formalities or not, and it crosses my mind that it's bad enough being inconvenienced by the living, without the dead getting on the act.

"We phoned the hospital mortuary." The undertaker rubs his hands together. "Asked them to check they had no unclaimed bodies, just in case…"

"What do they suggest we do?" I have decided to be a little more pro-active.

"All they could come up with was that we should check the label."

"The label?"

"On the body." He tugs at his sleeves, pulls them each one in turn neatly over the immaculate white cuffs of his shirt. "I'll have to get a screwdriver to get the coffin open."

The assistant trails behind him, and with her free hand accompanies the door to its jamb so that it closes without a sound. Down the corridor, her sneezing is at odds with the canned music of birds singing a new dawn, the brook lapping the shores of peace, and the soaring of the flute towards the sky which I imagine to be a blinding blue in preparation with a meeting with the Almighty.

Mr Evans hurries back.

He rests a hand on the lid of coffin, loosens one of the screws, and drops it in his jacket pocket.

127

"The body has been embalmed so it should not be unpleasant." He deals with the other four screws in turn, and the effort has him poke out a pink tongue. "The trouble these days," his tone is mournful, "is that death is no longer seen as part of living. I blame television and the lack of family life."

Quite how he links the two I'm not sure, and I am about to ask when the open casket reveals our mystery man, short-legged in black trousers, barefoot and thankfully, duly tagged with a label tied to his big toe.

I rummage inside my handbag, pull a tissue out of a small plastic pocket and blow my nose to cover the rising need to giggle. Nerves, of course, common at funerals but in my case it's more of a reaction to the serious dilemma I am facing as I can't very well identify the body unless I'm sure. And I'm not. Even with the name, date of birth and death printed black on the brown paper label, as if the poor man is nothing more than a vulgar package. How come he was so fat in life and so thin and shrunken in death? He looks like a "before and after" slimming advert in a cheap magazine.

A couple of deep breaths and I regain my composure. "Was there a wife or a girlfriend with him when he died?"

Mr Evans nods a couple of times. "Yes, a woman he's been living with. She's the one who told us he wanted to be buried in France in the family grave." He walks over to a small desk-like table in the corner and returns with a pale blue folder. "I gather he has a mother there, who lives in some small village near Nantes. They have been estranged ever since he left France. Nevertheless, I have asked our local police to contact their opposite numbers so that she will be informed, and be present at the airport should she wish to, when he is flown back.

Poor woman. I wonder what she will make of her son after a thirty year absence. Would she even know if she got sent the wrong one?

"What do you think we should do?" Mr Evans pops a mint in his mouth and I wish he had offered me one.

I'm not sure. My throat is dry, my blouse sticks to my skin, I need a few gulps of fresh air. I look at the window. Another fake. This time it is no more than a panel of coloured glass inserted in the wall and lit from behind, nothing to do with the sun, the rhythm of the day and the possibility of uncontaminated breathing.

A glance at the clock confirms that I am running late for my next appointment.

129

"I've got to make a call," I tell Mr Evans. I catch him biting his nails.

By the time I've been put through to the psychiatric unit where I am expected to attend a meeting to consider a young French woman patient's repatriation, and explain I am unlikely to make it by 12.30, the undertaker has buried both hands deep in his trouser pockets.

"If you are willing to take the risk I think we should go ahead." He looks sullen.

I take a deep breath. "You do know that he," I point at the coffin, "might be sent back if he's not who we hope him to be?"

Mr Evans swallows hard.

"It's happened before." I avoid looking at him. "And it is a rather unpleasant experience."

I fiddle with my pen and give him a few seconds to consider my remark. "Having said that… we've done all we can, and I can't see us being held responsible if the hospital made a mistake. Can you?"

I take his silence as an affirmative.

We face each other. He nods.

So be it.

From my "funeral case", a small Edwardian leather box I bought for pennies in a Bristol junk shop many years ago, I retrieve a short bar of red sealing wax, hunt around for the candle that should be there but is not, take out a disposable lighter and a black handled seal of the Republic; round, and no more than four inches in diameter, it offers the figure of Liberty wearing the same crown of seven arches as her oversized American cousin.

I pull a length of black ribbon out of my handbag - a good thing I remembered to replenish my stock last week - and scan the room for a flat surface where I might rest the tools of the grim task I am about to perform.

Mr Evans points to the table by the pretend window. "Would that do?"

I nod. "I'll need your help," I tell him, "if you don't mind."

He shuffles by my side.

I circle the coffin with a length of ribbon. "What I want you to do is hold the two ends together and remove your finger when I begin to drip the wax." I plant my right index on the short overlap I have created. "Like that."

He hesitates.

"Don't worry," I smile, "I haven't done any permanent damage as yet…"

But all he does is stare at his right hand as if trying to decide which finger he can sacrifice to the strange rite of passage he is about to witness.

131

Lack of practice - I am glad to say I don't have to do this too often - has me produce a smudge on the first attempt and I fail to attach the impression of the seal to the wax. Difficult to handle because it softens slowly, and hardens again in seconds. I scrape the metal clean with a coin I find in my pocket, set it down, return the hesitant flame of the lighter once more and wait for the end of the stick to turn gooey. I smell the pain before I feel it. It's my thumbnail going brown. I bite back a potent French swear word.

"Hold the ribbon in place," I am growing impatient with my unwilling assistant. Slowly the wax drips, puddles, darkens. I lower the seal, press hard, avoid Mr Evans' bony and shaky finger, only just.

I stand back. Not bad. I managed a clear picture of a diminutive *Liberté* trapped ready for the customs officers' scrutiny before the sealed coffin is allowed to be loaded onto the aircraft and flown to Paris, and later transferred to a van and the final journey to a small village in the Loire Atlantique.

Now to the rest of the formalities: paperwork. Complex, and there's no room for error.

I look around for a surface large enough for me to spread out the paperwork when Mr Evans suggests I might like to use his office, an offer I am happy to accept.

He leads the way.

Once there, he makes room on his desk, draws back the heavy chair, and angles it ready for me to sit down. I unfasten my briefcase, take out the various documents I need, spread them out on the green leather top, and get to work.

Somehow I miss a line halfway down one of the many forms I have to fill in, and have to start again. It takes me a while to locate the post-mortem and the sanitation certificate issued by the hospital and reunite them with the French translation, both of them filed away in the wrong folder. I double check the birth and the death certificate together with the permission for burial in the French cemetery.

The list goes on, and the whole process is taking longer than I'd expected.

I've signed the last of the documents. All that remains for me to do is wet the consular seal on the regulation purple ink pad, not too much or it might smudge, apply it with gentle force to both copies and originals, before selecting the ones that will accompany the deceased on his way back to France.

"If you are done," Mr Evans is by my side," I suggest we pay our final respects to the deceased."

Down the corridor to the Chapel of Rest for the last time.

I stand by the coffin of the man soon to be at rest in the country of his birth, and I send a silent prayer. This is a final goodbye, not an au revoir.

# For Your Eyes Only

*Operation Oyster Catcher was a routine exercise involving a number of emergency services. The objective: to test the response to a major terrorist incident in Wales.*

When asked on the 7th November, 2006 about the results of the exercise, the Secretary of State for the Home Department stated:

*"The results of the exercise will be fed into classified contingency plans for responding to a wide range of emergencies." www.Parliament.uk Column 1391 W*

Years later, much about the operation remains classified material, and although not bound by the Official Secrets Act, I was told to exercise caution when writing about what happened on that long weekend in October 2006.

No mention was made of my - very minor - contribution to the exercise.

Probably just as well.

As an abstract concept, taking part in an exercise shrouded in mystery was tempting for an avid reader of spy fiction, and it was not until I got out of the car for the very first briefing, late on a wet Friday evening, that I began to question the wisdom of my decision. So much information to take in, so many acronyms flying around (the majority meant nothing to me), the feeling I was treading water, and at risk of drowning in facts, figures and far-fetched hypotheses.

The exposé came to an end, the screen went blank.

"Any questions?" asked the man in charge.

I thought it best to leave it to my colleagues - both of them career consuls - to query a few points that would help me get a clearer picture of what to expect, but neither of them did.

"No, it's fine," they said, and smiled in unison. With a positive click, they retracted their biros, shuffled the pages of notes they'd made, dropped them in official looking briefcases, and stood, eager to proceed, or so it seemed to me.

"Obviously you will get all the help you need throughout the weekend," continued the official who had briefed us.

Down deserted corridors, a short ride in the lift, and our host invited us to climb into a black people carrier.

"I wish you luck."

The remark made me wince.

There was the slamming of doors, the purring of the powerful engine, the streetlights blurring in the rain through the tinted windows, and we were on our way to an unknown destination.

It wasn't until we reached the Police Headquarters in Carmarthen that the size of the operation began to dawn on me. Our headlamps picked out bustling shadows across the car park. As my eyes got used to the darkness, the silhouettes turned into men and women; they wore uniforms, from the dark blue of the police force to the light green of nurses, the yellow oilskins of firemen, and here and there, others I couldn't make out in the gloom.

Our ID papers were scrutinised, questions asked, and passes clipped to our lapels. A near-automated looking young police officer ushered us into the main building. There was something of a warren about the place: corridors heading in all directions, unmarked doors, and a flow of uniformed men and women hurrying past who clutched coloured paper files to their chests, whispered in budlike microphones nestling in the palm of their hands, and I couldn't but envy their sense of purpose.

By contrast there was nothing for my two colleagues and me to do but stand in the draughty corridor, and wait.

And wait some more.

"Right," said one of them after a long while, "I've had enough of this hanging around. Let's find somewhere to sit down, and if the powers that be need our help they'll have to find us."

In silence we followed him in search of a room, down the corridors that twisted and turned, and forced us to double back on ourselves a couple of times. It wasn't until he'd tried half a dozen door handles that he found a room that hadn't been locked. We stepped inside, pulled chairs away from the large meeting table, and settled on the cold plastic seats in mild discomfort. The lack of heating didn't improve our mood.

We'd been sitting down in silence for some twenty minutes when the door was pushed open.

"There you are."

A high ranking police officer - judging by the gold stripes on his jacket sleeves - hurried inside, acknowledged each of us in turn with a short bow, cleared his throat, and looked at his watch.

"I am sorry to have to report that, some two hours ago, at 2100 hours, a ferry bound for Ireland was hijacked off the coast of France. As yet no group has claimed responsibility for such an action."

"I take it the passengers and crew are held hostage?" asked one of my colleagues.

"How many people involved?" asked the other.

"Difficult to say at this stage. We are doing all we can to get hold of the ship's manifest."

My two colleagues turned to each other, eyebrows raised, and engaged in a short verbal duet.

"You can't be serious."

"I don't believe it."

"This isn't good enough."

"Never heard of such a thing."

"Surely, the manifest should be available by now."

The police official retreated towards the door, and left us with the promise that he would keep us up to date with further developments.

More waiting. We paced up and down the room, ventured in the corridor hoping to garner some fresh information, all the while complaining that this was no way to treat members of the Consular Corps.

Finally, and with a great show of irritation, my colleagues flicked their mobile phones open, and dialled the Home Office, or so I gathered from the brief exchanges that followed, in which both consuls made clear to whoever was listening that they resented being kept in the dark.

"And I don't care if the Home Secretary has to be dragged out of an official dinner," shouted one of them, "we are talking national security here so get him to call me back."

They then made a show of calling their respective ambassadors, none too happy apparently, to hear that significant facts, such as the numbers and the identity of their nationals held hostage still had not been made available.

3 hours since the hijacking had taken place.

And still no information and nothing for us to do, but watch the wall clock.

"I'm cold," announced one of my colleagues. "I think we could do with a hot drink and something to eat. Heaven knows what the rest of the night is going to be like."

Back to the maze of corridors in search of the cafeteria. Not easy to find; no tell-tale cooking smells, no clinking cutlery, no loud voices, just a discreet sign on a half glazed door we could easily have missed.

As soon as we sat down at one of the many empty tables, a woman in a pink tabard hurried towards us, busied herself with the laminated menu cards she slotted back in their wooden stands.

"No point looking at those, we've only lasagne left." She gave the table a quick wipe, stared at each one of us in turn and asked, "Actors are you?"

I must have misheard. "Actors?" I asked.

She shrugged her shoulders, looked a little disappointed.

To my surprise neither of my colleagues picked up on the brief exchange.

"We are no actors," I said. "We are Consuls, here to represent 3 different countries."

"Never mind," she replied, "no doubt the actors will come later tonight when you turn in."

I was about to ask what she meant when a police officer rushed in and pointed to the large television screen in the corner of the room.

"You'd better watch that," he jutted his chin towards me. "More complications for the French it seems."

From where I was sitting I struggled to make sense of the newsflash, of the looped ribbon of typed words running along the bottom of the screen alive with a game show.

*Terrorists have set fire to the French refinery near…* it read *there is fear of many casualties. More threats issued by terrorists as yet not identified.*

141

"You might want to call your Consul General," suggested one of my colleagues. "He should be able to tell you what to do."

I dialled the private number. Waited. No answer. "This is urgent. Could you please call me back, as soon as you pick up this message?" And tell me what to do, I added but was too embarrassed to speak the words aloud.

For all that they looked annoyed, and complained at the continuing lack of news, my colleagues chatted amiably and didn't look particularly anxious. By contrast I couldn't help but picture the hostages - men, women and children - cold, hungry, terrified, silent, waiting.

So powerful were the images, so realistic the atmosphere in which we were immersed, so plausible the facts presented to us that I lost sight we were no more than players in a high powered exercise.

It was gone midnight by the time we were driven to a local hotel. And still no update.

After barely 4 hours sleep, the loud ringing of the alarm call forced me out of bed. Once showered and dressed, I staggered into the dining room to share the pre-packed breakfast of the early risers - not a category I usually belong to - with my two colleagues.

We just had time to collect our bags before being hurried into a police car; down a winding road at speed, a sharp descent towards the sea, some harsh braking, and we reached the quayside, where we battled against the wind to push the car doors open.

The sky melted with the white crested waves; they swelled, rolled towards us, slammed against the jetty, and exploded into thick spray. There was the taste of salt on my lips, the smell of rotting seaweed and the cold, biting through my lightweight coat. I shivered.

"Don't worry about the weather conditions," I'd been told, "there shouldn't be any need for you to be outside." I should have followed my instinct, and wrapped up in proper winter clothing.

I'm not sure how long we stood in the wind and icy rain, waiting for news of the hostages, shortly to be released, but I remember looking for shelter whilst my colleagues hunted, yet again, for someone in the know.

That's when I saw her.

She sat on a small stone wall overlooking the harbour. Her hair was a mess, her clothes crumpled as if she had slept fully dressed; she had lost a shoe, and I wondered what she was doing in an

143

area designated – or so we'd been told - as a high security zone.

*"Aidez-moi s'il vous plaît."*

I looked around. Nobody but her and me. I took a few steps towards her. *Je m'appelle Christine j'ai 10 ans. J'ai perdu mes parents,* read the message written in bold letters on a large piece of card dangling from a piece of string looped round her neck.

*"Vous étiez sur le bateau?"* I asked, but got no reply. If she'd been on the boat what was she doing here?

I couldn't fathom why a grown woman claimed to be ten and have lost her parents, but whatever the reason she shouldn't been sitting outside in the cold. She recoiled when I reached out for her hand, and it was obvious I wouldn't make progress on my own.

*"Cinq minutes."* I held my right hand up and stretched out my fingers. *"Je reviens dans cinq minutes."*

I went for help, only to be met with indifference, a shrug of the shoulders, averted looks, from those I approached, uniformed or not. I was running out of time. She'd been worried, wondering if I would return. My only hope was to locate my colleagues. They might know what to do, or at least give me some advice.

No sooner had I caught up with them, and before I had a chance to explain about the strange woman who pretended to be a child, that they rushed me towards but yet another car, told me to hurry, bundled me in and we were driven away at speed.

"Some actions at last," said one of my colleagues.

News had apparently filtered through that the hijacking had been resolved by security forces, that the hostages were on their way to the local comprehensive school, and that we would be allowed to see them and bring any help they might need.

"About time," complained the other one. "I want to know how the authorities will justify keeping us in the dark for so long. It's totally unacceptable."

And unacceptable it might have been but there was no time to dwell on the rights and wrongs of the situation. Buses were pulling up outside the school.

Huddled in their coats but shivering still, dishevelled, faces drawn, eye sockets bruised through lack of sleep, the hostages emerged, climbed out of the vehicles and in small clumps stumbled inside the large school hall. There was little talking. They queued for hot drinks and food, and were invited by volunteers to regroup around the refectory tables according to their nationalities.

Busy looking for French nationals I failed to notice the man who ran in. He tapped me on the shoulder.

"We need you to translate, please follow me to the medical room. Hurry."

From then on, when I try and recall what happened, images stutter, as they do on old black and white film; I watch myself rushing up and down the school corridors, hurrying back and forth from the medical room to the main hall where I am needed to translate, consulting list after list of names, all in an attempt to locate the possible French citizens I am here to help. It doesn't matter how many times I count and double check, I am always short. It's mainly children who are missing.

What I do remember clearly, however, is the woman who walked into the room I'd been given as a temporary office. There was something of the civil servant about her, the dark suit, the black attaché case and the no-nonsense glasses.

"Have you considered there might be such a thing as virtual players involved in the exercise?" she said as she stood in front of my desk.

"Virtual as not real, is that what you mean?"

A brief nod. "Bear it in mind. I believe you would find the concept very helpful." A brief smile and she walked away.

Surely I would have been told.

My thoughts turned to my two colleagues and the likely possibility they had been briefed when I hadn't, and not shared their knowledge with me. I sat and stared again at the list of names I'd been given. Fictional or real, how was I supposed to know?

I had no choice but to go through the motions, keep up the pretence. I commiserated with the passengers I was responsible for, checked their IDs, offered advice on the best way to get home or resume their interrupted journey, knowing all the while that my participation was flawed, and my efforts futile.

Relief came at last when coaches pulled up outside the school and the hostages - duly processed, or so we were led to believe - climbed on board to be taken to the train stations and airports of their choice.

The exercise was over.

147

I was drained, and had nothing to contribute to the lively exchange between my two colleagues as to the importance of planning for the possibility of a terrorist attack on our way back to HQ.

Dusk was falling by the time the car pulled up out outside the main building. A police officer rushed to open the door.

"The Chief Constable wondered if you'd like to have a look at the operations room."

Judging by the eagerness of my colleagues I was the only one in a hurry to be going home, to a hot bath, a numbing television programme and a good night's sleep. Still, it would be churlish not to accept the invitation, and I doubted there was that much to see. It wouldn't take long.

"Follow me, please."

We trailed behind him, down a narrow footpath tunnelled by panels of thick green material that flapped with the rising wind, and kept us from view.

Nobody spoke.

We reached a tall metal door.

Waited.

There was the clicking of a lock being released from the inside.

A panel slid opened to reveal a space so vast, so unexpected, I faltered before stepping inside. No windows, bare walls, high ceiling, and the standard metal girders of a rudimentary sports hall.

Turned war room.

Coloured lights flashed on wall maps, computer screens flickered, phones buzzed, printers hummed. Our escort pointed to civilians and members of the three forces rushing from one area to the other.

"Coordination is key at every level, and of course there's more going on behind the scenes."

The whole placed throbbed with energy so intense, a sense of urgency so deep, I found it almost impossible to accept there'd been no hijacking, no emergency, and no threat to innocent lives.

At last the time came to leave headquarters and the world of make believe. I shook hands with my two colleagues, climbed into the police car that was to take me home and wondered how long it would take me to come to terms with my inability to separate truth from fiction.

*With grateful thanks to Dr Wyn Price, Head of Resilience, Welsh Government.*

# Unexpected Sprouting

With a busy weekend ahead I had planned on a leisurely Friday morning. I would block incoming calls, indulge in a long soak, attend to my face and hands, have some much needed me time.

At first I ignored the doorbell, assumed it was the postman. Either he would call again or else, and I sighed at the thought, I would have to retrieve the Special Delivery letter from the far away depot where they always insist on checking my ID - very French.

The bell rang again, insistent, screeching almost.

I let out a few expletives - in my mother tongue, more satisfying than in English - put my hands over my ears but the noise would not go away. In the end I had no choice but to haul myself out of the bath, slip on a robe, pad downstairs with wet feet, and push the bolt open.

"Yes?" I almost barked at the woman who stood in the porch, her hand still on the bell pull.

*"Vous êtes le consul de France?"* Her anger deflated my irritation.

"Yes the *Honorary* Consul." I often have to reinstate the adjective, usually to no avail. She certainly didn't seem to have heard me.

"I've just had my handbag stolen." Her French carried the flavour of the Mediterranean south. She pushed past me and stepped over the threshold. "What are you going to do about it?"

Aware, that in my state of undress I was no match for an aggressive woman and, fearing more than a verbal attack, I tightened the knot on my robe, took a few steps back, and manoeuvred my visitor towards the consular room.

"Do take a seat. I shan't be long. If you'll excuse me..."

I rushed upstairs, where, with no concern for style or colour coordination, pulled trousers and a jumper out of my wardrobe, got dressed, brushed my hair, and addressed an itchy ear in front of the bathroom mirror. Still seething, but feeling better equipped to cope with the woman's invasion I made my way downstairs. There, she was pacing my room and refused to sit down when I put it to her that form filling would be easier if she were to take a seat.

"Forms? What forms? I've already given all the details at the police station before they told me I had to come and see you."

151

"And that was the right thing to do, but you now need to inform the French authority, and once you have completed this document," I pushed it towards her, it will go to the Consulate to make sure you don't fall prey to ID thieves."

"I see." Her voice had softened a little.

"I'll keep a copy and give you another one to send to your insurance company." I handed her a pen. "Shall we make a start?

She took a seat but as she did so, she gave me what can best be described as a strange look. I pretended not to notice, and suggested she made every effort to remember what she'd had stolen. It was an upsetting list: credit cards, driving license, passport, national health card, house keys, diary, 200 euros and as many pounds.

"I only had enough for a taxi to come to you, but I won't be able to pay for my hotel."

"I'll help you sort out a money transfer in the morning."

"But I've got no ID left."

"We'll go together and use mine. Don't worry I've done it before."

A cup of tea - the British panacea to many an ailment - and two digestive biscuits later and her mood had improved.

"I've no idea how it happened," she said. "I left the hotel just before nine to avoid the crowds. I bought three cashmere jumpers in M&S for my daughters - real bargains - and decided to go to the coffee shop and get a proper breakfast before doing any more shopping. I normally go to London, but it's so busy and exhausting I thought I'd give it a miss this year."

She added that she had found a good hotel and flight package on the internet. "And I never thought I would be at risk in a place like Cardiff." She took a deep breath and resumed her story. "One minute my bag was on the chair next to mine, and when I reached out to get my glasses to sort out my change, nothing, the seat was empty. I thought it might have fallen to the floor and that someone had kicked it under the banquette in front of me. I squatted down to look. It wasn't there. When I asked around nobody remembered seeing it."

"Did you notice anyone hovering by your table while you were eating?"

"No, and I think I would have because the coffee shop wasn't that busy." She stared at her feet, ran her fingers along the hem of her skirt, dug deep into her coat pocket and blew her nose into a pink handkerchief. "I still can't believe it happened. The staff were very helpful, and so was the police when I went to report the theft, but they didn't think I was likely to get anything back."

By the time we had completed the form filling - in triplicate (with the help of carbon paper) in the case of a loss/ or theft of documents; a true anachronism at the age of emails and computers - I was tempted to ask her about the puzzlement on her face when she looked at me. Had we met before? Did I strongly resemble someone she knew?

I didn't feel I could ask.

We made arrangements to meet the next day before I called her a taxi that would take her back to her hotel.

"Thank you for your help. *A demain.*" She shook my hand, kept her gaze averted, which I found odd.

Until I reached the bathroom, and came face to face with my reflection in the mirror. I would have to explain.

That I didn't usually conduct consular business in my dressing gown, with a cotton bud sprouting from my left ear, or the right one, come to think of it.

# My New Mobile Phone

It's not for me, that round robin New Year SMS that clogs up the networks on the 31$^{st}$ of December. I much prefer the personal touch when expressing my best wishes to family, friends and acquaintances.

Bound to prove a little challenging this year, however, as my old mobile died on me days before the beginning of my winter break and I've had no choice but to accept an upgrade from my provider.

"It's a great phone, you'll get used to it in no time, believe me." I have no doubt as to the sincerity of the young salesman, but I do question my ability to transfer a few basic skills over to the thinner, larger, faster mobile nestling in its box and ready to go.

Come New Year's Eve I have mastered the new screen, the arrows, the contact box, and I feel brave enough to text my daughter.

*Darling, hope you have a great year ahead, all the best with whatever you do. Love you, always.*

A row of kisses and it's ready to go.

A brief hesitation as I consider which sending option to select - of course I want to send

155

all of the message, so, a little pressure from my index finger on the shiny black pad and it's done.

I do feel a little smug.

"Are you ready?"

"Give me two minutes," I tell my husband, adding that it won't take us long to climb the two flights of stairs to the neighbours with whom we shall see in the New Year.

"Got the gift?"

"On the hall table."

"House keys?"

"In the door."

"Mobile phone?"

"Won't be needing it."

It's a fun evening. Plenty of Champagne, lovely food, and we don't get home until the early hours of the morning. Needless to say we were straight to bed, later than usual to get up, and enjoyed a leisurely New Year's Day breakfast.

"I heard your phone tinkle," announces my husband from the living room.

"Yes, I know. It can wait." I have more important things to see to, like a second cup of strong coffee.

"Listen, it's done it again." He brings me the phone.

I rest it in the palm of my hand, and feel it vibrate, seconds before the mechanical chirping heralds a volley of messages.

I pat the screen back to life, and open the message box.

"That's odd."

"What does it say?"

"Thank you,' I read. 'So good to know how you truly feel.'

"And look at the number of crosses."

"Depends who it's from."

"The Consul General."

My husband looks a little aback. "What do you think he meant?"

I am too busy scrolling down to the next message to offer a reply.

"Oh!"

"What's the matter?"

His turn to read aloud, "*I had not suspected the depth of your feelings dear Claude see you soon. X* And the sender is. . ."

"I'm not sure I want to know."

"There's a surprise. It's from the Ambassador."

And there is more: a message from HMS Cambria, another from a member of the Welsh government, followed by texts sent by the Lord

Mayor, police contacts, a couple of journalists, consular colleagues, my dentist… the list goes on, everyone expressing surprise and displaying various levels of humour in their reply.

All except one in which the sender takes pains to criticise the tone of my message, describing it as over-personal, unsuitable and not befitting my position.

"What message does JF refer to, whoever he is?"

"I've no idea."

"Can't you go back and have a look at them?"

"There's only been the one. I thought I'd deal with the others later today."

"What did it say?"

"It was to Carolyn, wishing her a great year, you know, the usual. It couldn't have anything to do with. . ."

I wonder.

I remember my slight hesitation when asked if I wanted to send the whole message before pressing ALL. Unless. . .

Unless it had meant ALL as in contacts, in which case…

My face is burning. The shame. The thought of weeks of having 'Love you, darling' quoted at me. I feel such a fool.

"Are you alright?"

I'll have to tell my worried husband. But right now all I can do is press hard on the off button and silence my mobile for the next few hours.

# Short, Short Stories

### Size Matters

*"Ici le Ministère de l'agriculture et de la pèche maritime, un de nos bateaux est en difficulté."*

"Sorry to hear that, where is the boat?"

"Off the Welsh coast, and I was told that you..."

"Sorry to interrupt, but I don't usually deal with fishing related problems. You should speak to my colleague in Swansea."

"I believe he is away."

"Yes, but he'll be back in a couple of days."

"I'm afraid it can't wait."

"An accident?"

"No, nothing like that, thank goodness."

"Better tell me what's happened and I'll see if there is anything I can do to help."

"As you may know there are strict EU regulations when it comes to the use of fishing nets."

"I didn't know, and I told you I'm not the one to talk to about fishing matters."

"Well, the captain of one of our trawlers has been found using the wrong size nets."

"To catch more fish?"

"I can't say."

"Hm… and?"

"He has been summoned to appear in court tomorrow and will need a solicitor."

"I shouldn't worry about that, he will automatically be entitled to legal representation. Does he speak English?"

"Not much, just enough to get by."

"In that case he has the right to a translator."

"That's good, but how do we go about finding one?"

"There's bound to be an accredited one in the Swansea area. I'll have a look at the official list on the consular website."

"Failing that is there any chance you could…?"

"No, I'm sorry, a translator has to remain impartial, and under the circumstances it could easily be argued that there is a clear case of conflict of interest. It wouldn't be allowed."

"I see. Is there any chance you could drive over anyway? For moral support if nothing else."

"Where would I find him?"

"He's moored at Haverfordwest. Or it could be Milford Haven."

"You're not sure?"

"No, sorry, we've been having terrible communication problems."

"But you did speak to him?"

"The call was very short, kept breaking up."

"And the name of the trawler?"

"The name, yes. Well… I should have it confirmed shortly. We've got three of them in the area. It does complicate matters."

I let the silence hang for a few seconds.

"If I've understood you correctly, you want me to drive some 200km to an uncertain destination for a friendly chat with a man on board a trawler whose name you are not sure of?"

"If you put it that way."

"Can you think of another?"

*PAUSE.*

"You won't be coming then?"

"It's out of the question, sorry."

There was the faintest of clicks as I laid the phone back to rest.

## Timing

*"Madame le Consul Honoraire*, a question please before I bring the meeting to a close."

"Of course."

"As you know *le Président de la République* will be leaving the Millennium Stadium shortly before the end of the match so as to avoid the crowds, and driven straight back to Rhoose airport.

"Yes, so I gather."

"How long would you say it will take for him to be driven back to the presidential plane?"

"It will depend."

"What do you mean?"

"The traffic is likely to be heavy and…"

"What traffic?"

"Think official motorcade," whispers a colleague sitting next to me, "think police outriders."

"Sorry," I tell the head of the French President's visit preparatory mission. I didn't think. . ."

Too late.

It's the look he gives me, just before slotting me into the slow-witted category.

## Failing to please.  Again.

"My husband and I bought a plot of land at the foot of the Pyrénées with the intention of building a straw house, and I need some advice."

"I'm afraid that all I know about straw houses is what happened when the big bad wolf blew down the little pig's house."

"I appreciate not everybody is into alternative lifestyles, but all I want is some help with the regulations governing such builds.  For instance when it comes to the *réglementation thermique* – to do with heat loss I take it - how do we set about finding an *organisme certificateur reconnu par l'état?"*

"I take it you looked it up on the internet?"

"Of course, we did, but it's no use, it's far too complicated, I can't make head nor tail of the information."

"Oh dear!"

"And what about the *DPE*, and the *ALUR* law, and. . ."

"May I suggest you get in touch with the local Mairie. They should be able to help."

"I did, but they don't have any English."

"Really?  Well, I suppose you could contact a translator."

"Far too expensive.  I was hoping you could have a word with the Conseil Municipal, after all you are French, it wouldn't be a problem for you."

"I can't do that."

"I can't see why not. I thought your role was to help people."

"It is, but I'm afraid acting as translator of building regulations to someone who wants to build a house made of straw is way outside my remit."

The click of the receiver going down was bursting with indignation.

# About the Author

Brought up in Paris, Claude Annik Rapport has now spent longer in Wales than in her home country.

An Alumni of Cardiff University, she had a varied teaching career before being appointed as Honorary Consul for France, based in the Welsh capital, where she was in post for 16 years. She describes her time in this role as fascinating and highly rewarding.

To this day, the author remains very much involved with the French community.

In recognition of her services to France she was made a *chevalier de l'Ordre National du Mérite* and awarded the *Légion d'Honneur*.

Her work has appeared in literary magazines and anthologies, and she is currently putting together a collection of short stories, due to be published in 2018.

She lives in Cardiff with her husband Anthony.

**Photograph Credit:** *Nathalie Garin Weston*

86630837R00096

Made in the USA
Columbia, SC
17 January 2018